Cover Photographs:

Front cover:
On the Equator, Catequilla, Ecuador
Back Cover:
Preparing for The State Visit, Budapest

Dustjacket only:
Inside front flap:
Her Majesty's Address to the Hungarian Parliament
Back Flap:
The Olmecoid Heads at La Democracia, Guatemala

For Gillian Angrave

A personal insight, told with warmth and humour, into a remarkable career spent in a variety of countries around the world. A fascinating story, with Gillian's love for travel and for her work apparent throughout. I did not want this book to end.

Literary Review

Gillian's whirlwind tour of the world sweeps us off on posting after posting with the FCO.

Her take is of an independent woman who took on the world and made it her own. Her story serves as a timely reminder of just how much strong women like her have shaped the world for us all.

Lydia Maxwell, Editor
CAROUSEL
The Diplomatic Service Families Association

Youngsters in the market for a little career inspiration should look no further than 'Skirting the World' for its depiction of a rich and varied life of travel. Even the youngest and most web-hardened digital native cannot fail to fall for its allure. Some might even follow in Gillian's footsteps.

Sarah Robinson, Senior Journalist,
Nautilus International

A fantastic book. I couldn't stop reading it. I loved all the details of Gillian's work and travels, and of hearing about the life of an amazing lady.

Ian Morrison

BOOKS BY THE SAME AUTHOR

'From Oceans to Embassies'

Venice: The Diary of an Awestruck Traveller

Volume 1:

From Swamp to La Serenissima

Volume 2:

Betwixt and Between

Volume 3:

Hidden Gems

Volume 4:

Precious Yet Precarious

About the Author
Gillian (Gill) Angrave

Born in Leicester in 1945, Gillian was educated at Guthlaxton Grammar School and the Leicester College of Technology. After three years working in Leicester as a PA for an architect, an engineering company, and The Rank Organization, she joined P&O as an Assistant Purser in 1967, sailing in CANBERRA and ORIANA until 1974.

After a brief spell ashore, she again got 'itchy feet' and in 1976 joined the Foreign & Commonwealth Office as Ambassador's PA, a position she held and greatly enjoyed until her retirement in 2005. Her postings took her to the Philippines, Peru, Guatemala, Chile, Mexico and Hungary.

Single, her love of travel somehow always seemed to get in the way of marriage. Upon her retirement, however, she became a Registrar of Marriages in West Sussex, a job she also loves and still continues. Now she marries everyone else!

Gillian's hobbies include Tai Chi, travel, photography, modern languages, bell-ringing, golf; and, of course, writing.

Gillian Angrave

Skirting the World

My Life as an Ambassador's PA

Craig House Books
Chichester

First published in Great Britain by Craig House Books in 2023.
Copyright © Gillian Angrave 2023.

The right of Gillian Angrave to be identified as the author of this work has been asserted by her in accordance with the Copyright, Designs and Patents Act 1988.

A CIP catalogue record of this book can be obtained from the British Library

Hardback   ISBN 978-1-7392983-02   (First Edition)
Paperback   ISBN 978-1-7392983-40   (First Edition)

Book designed and typeset by Gillian Angrave
Cover designed by Cottagewebs

Printed and bound in Great Britain by ImprintDigital.com, Upton Pyne, Exeter, Devon.

Disclaimer:

www.gillangrave.co.uk
info@gillianangrave.co.uk

To my sister, Sheila,
With much love

CONTENTS

Preface

Be Inspiring, Be Original, Be Loyal, Be Yourself.

I've always tried to live by these values, though whether or not I've succeeded, only others can say. But I'm aware that I've been very fortunate to have lived a life that many people can only dream of and trying to explain what it is or has been like has not always been easy or appreciated. I'm conscious people may think I'm boasting, or blowing my own trumpet, but this is just the way my life has turned out.

A large part of this life has been spent as a Civil Servant working for the Foreign & Commonwealth Office. Twenty-nine years and nine months to be exact. I feel a great affection for, pride in, and loyalty to this Government Department. I have had the privilege of working for and with some exceptionally talented role models, and for this I am very grateful. They, and the Diplomatic Service in general, have given me so much and have been instrumental in molding me into the person I am today.

However, this is not to say that life with The Office has always been a bed of roses. It has not. And since this is my story, I shall, on occasions, as tactfully and respectfully as possible, say so. As my favourite Ambassador [Sir] John Birch in Budapest, wrote in a review for me of '*From Oceans to Embassies*' – "Gillian has a kind and lucid pen", and I have been anxious to adhere to this throughout the writing of this book.

Sadly, John died at the beginning of the pandemic. I owe him so much for his advice, guidance and support whilst I was frantically putting pen to paper for my memoir, and I miss him a lot. I hope he is looking down now and nodding with approval at the result of this, my latest endeavour.

As well as to my sister, this book is dedicated to him, but also to all those with whom I worked, whether still with us or not. All I can say is – a heartfelt thank you.

"Live your life like a butterfly:
take a rest sometimes, but always
remember to fly.

PART ONE

Destined to Travel

Chapter One

My Wanderlust Begins

I should have been a Monarch butterfly, I've decided, flying long distances, settling, then off again. This sums up my life very nicely!

I was destined to travel. In 1948, a Romany gypsy knocked at our front door clutching a heavy woven basket full of heather and dolly pegs, entreating Mum to buy. We were not at all well off, but Mum felt sorry for this wizened old lady and went to find a thruppenny piece to give her to buy six dolly pegs.

"Shall I read your fortune"?", croaked the gypsy. Mum nodded, secretly fearing it might cost more, but unwilling to have a spell cast on her, as was the myth at that time.

"You will have two daughters. One will be musical, and one will go over the seas" was all she said as she trudged wearily down the path.

I was three at the time and was out of sight playing in the back garden. My sister, Sheila, was born a year later. Mum was intrigued by this prophecy but thought nothing more of it and went back to her chores. However, years later, when I joined the merchant navy and Sheila became a flautist, Mum realized, much to her great amazement, that the gypsy's prediction had in fact been fulfilled. Even more so when, on leaving the sea, after a brief spell ashore I subsequently took up a career with the Diplomatic Service and kept on travelling. Looking back, all very spooky really,

I will never know what prompted that diminutive lady to utter those words all those years ago, but I for one have been eternally grateful to her for unknowingly and unwittingly charting the course my life was to take.

Sheila and me, October 1949

From Ship to Shore

Before I joined the Diplomatic Service as Ambassador's PA in 1976, this butterfly had opened her wings and had indeed embarked on a career 'over the seas' as an Assistant Purser with P&O from 1967 to 1974. I loved both these careers equally as I skirted the world, even though they were quite different.

My time at sea was special. The technical side of ships fascinates me to this day, and I worked hard to gain my Steering and Lifeboat Certificates. But it was the great camaraderie on board, amongst Officers and crew alike, that was so unique. It was hard work, and we often worked very long hours, but we had such fun, especially as we, the ship's company, in addition to our normal jobs, put on the entertainment for the passengers. In those days, before the advent of the jumbo jet, our voyages were mostly mainline, with few cruises, so there were rarely any professional artists travelling with us.

Carrying red roses aboard
ORIANA in SYDNEY in 1973

Roaring Forties Night, ORIANA

But all good things come to an end (or so I thought). As Women Assistant Pursers, we had to retire when we reached forty, with no pension arrangements, and I knew that this could never be considered a long-term career. I hated to leave my ships and shipmates, and was dragged very reluctantly, kicking and screaming, from P&O's **ORIANA** in 1974, to prepare myself for a life ashore.

But it was not to be. I soon got itchy feet and longed to be off again. I cast around for opportunities that would provide a long-term career of travel, and The Foreign Office seemed a good place to start. So, I filled in the application form and sent it off, with fingers tightly crossed that I would at least be considered. I was elated t h e r e f o r e w h e n a few weeks later, I received a letter inviting me to go down to London for an interview. I met all the criteria and passed the interview with flying colours, I was informed. I went home full of optimism and a few days later received a letter confirming my appointment as a PA in the Diplomatic Service. I couldn't have been happier.

It was July 1976, and I was working in Newcastle at the time. I packed up and drove to London to live temporarily in the Civil Service hostel in Gloucester Road as I had nowhere else to stay. Mum and Dad were proud that I had landed such a prestigious job, even if it meant me going away again, but as I was to find throughout the whole of my travelling career, this was the major downside – spending so long away from them, and the rest of my family and friends. It was the price I had to pay. They understood, though I know it was so hard for them too. We shed many a tear between us on numerous occasions as they saw me off from Birmingham airport, the nearest one to where they were living in Shropshire, knowing that we wouldn't see each other again for eighteen months, or two and a half years, or however long depending on where I was going.

Still, this is what the gypsy had predicted, and this is what I had chosen to do. And so - time to put away the well-worn Discharge Book and head off to pastures new. The world was my oyster yet again, and I was about to begin the next exciting chapter of my itinerant life.

PART TWO

The Foreign and Commonwealth Office

The Foreign and Commonwealth Office
King Charles, Street, London SW1A 2AH

The Grand Staircase

The Locarno Room

Chapter Two

A Brief Background

A Brief Background

Before I embark on my own life in the Diplomatic Service, a few words about the role of the Foreign and Commonwealth Office. The history of Britain and her Empire is complex, controversial and, at times very colourful, and The FCO, as it is colloquially known, has been at the heart of shaping that history. Whether one agrees with His Majesty's Government (HMG) or not, there is no doubt that we have been and still are, though perhaps to a lesser extent these days, a major player on the world stage and a force for good, not always appreciated at the time, but vital nonetheless. Much of this work has been carried out behind closed doors. This is true diplomacy, and whilst it may seem as if nothing is being accomplished, believe me behind the scenes is a very dedicated and talented team working furiously to achieve our goals. Diplomats are swans *par excellence*!

Being a part of this whirlwind existence is the reason why I value my time with The Office so much. It was a whole new world for me: one filled, whether at home or abroad, with non-stop hustle and bustle; of endless streams of foreign dignitaries, Royalty, eminent Government Ministers, and Heads of State - people I had previously only seen on the television or in the newspapers. I got to meet them, and I never stopped learning from these encounters.

Our London 'Home'

As if all this wasn't enough, there is that magnificent building in which I worked when in London, without doubt one of the finest in the world. It occupies the whole of the block from the north side of King Charles Street to Downing Street, with the Treasury opposite. I only went into their building once. Nice, but nothing like ours, but then "austerity begins at home" I always say. They never missed a chance to point this out to us: now it's my turn.

The Foreign Office was built in 1868 by George Gilbert Scott, working alongside Matthew Digby Wyatt, the surveyor of the East India Company, who designed the India Office part of the building. It was originally designed to accommodate four major Government Departments: The Foreign Office; the India Office, later incorporating the Colonial Office; and the Home Office until it moved into its own premises in 1978. It only survives to this day after prolonged and bitter in-fighting (no doubt mainly with the Treasury!).

As soon as I walked under the arch into our main Quadrangle, my heart never failed to skip a beat with sheer pride and awe at working in such illustrious and magnificent surroundings. And which foreign Ambassador could not fail to be impressed by the grandeur of the Grand Staircase as they entered through the Main Entrance, even if they had been summoned and were about to be hauled over the coals!

On my last home posting, when I was working for the Director (Under-Secretary of State) Wider Europe, I used to meet the Russian Ambassador, Karasin, and his First Secretary who accompanied him, at the Main Entrance when he had a meeting with my boss. Ambassador Karasin always remarked upon what a stunning building The Office was, in particular the Grand Staircase. He was a bear of a man, with a deep, sexy (to me) voice, and was always very pleasant and courteous. I looked forward to seeing him, even if his country was on the naughty step - again. I wish, though, that I could have spoken Russian to understand what was being said when I escorted him and his First Secretary in the lift back to the quadrangle after his meetings! But then he would have 'researched' me and known that I wasn't a Russian-speaker. Mind you, I could have surreptitiously attended night school to learn that language, but he would have known that too! I learned very early on that senior PAs were ideal candidates for the 'honey trap'!

The public rooms throughout the whole of the Foreign Office building are truly stunning: the Locarno Room, the India Office Council Chamber; the Foreign Secretary's office; and the Durbar Court, to name but a few. However, I remember when I first joined The Office, the Durbar Court was full of portacabins which acted as a Communications Centre. It was only during the main refurbishment from 1986-1994 that the Court was revealed in all its splendour.

In my time, and probably now too, even in our less than grand offices on the upper floors, you would find beautiful fireplaces (some of them Adam), old fashioned baths (which I used once when going out to the theatre one evening), and ancient plumbing, which thumped and clanged periodically. Fortunately, it was no longer the 'lot' of the lowly Grade 10s (nor PAs for that matter) to fill the coal skuttles and keep the fires going!

And you went from the old Colonial Office into the Foreign Office part through the "hole in the wall" – just that, only wide enough for one person to pass through at a time. Trying to find it, though, was a Herculean task.

There was also an antiquated system of distribution, installed in the 1940s, using Tubes, which whooshed past you at a great rate of knots, landing with a loud thud in your office if the communication was meant for your boss (amazing how they sent it down the right Tube). Sadly, all that has been replaced by emails, but I loved it, even if the noise was a bit disconcerting at times and it meant more work for me! Bring back the good old Tubes, I say.

Dead or Alive – Wildlife at the FCO!

In addition to the customary resident rats and mice, there was, and still is, *Albert*, that most revered and important member of the Diplomatic Service. Albert, presumably named after Queen Victoria's much-loved husband, is the **Diplomatic Anaconda**, presented to The Office by a Guyanese Bishop around 1892. I'm not certain I'd be flattered to have a snake named after me, but then who am I to merit such an honour? **_Albert_** stretches the whole width of one of the Library end walls and has recently been the centre of some controversy as he's just been re-stuffed at a cost of £10,000. Good for him! He's very long and quite thick (in the physical sense), so personally I wouldn't quibble too much over the price. Value for money, I reckon. Given my fear of snakes, I love him like a hole in the head, but I couldn't bear to see him go. Whenever I went into the Library, I could never sit under him at that end, nor could I look at him from the other end. I didn't spend much time in the Library!

Looking good, *Albert*!

Our Diplomatic Falcons

But it gets better. As befits such an illustrious Government Department as ours, we at the FCO have our very own **falconer,** complete with two, not one, beautiful **Diplomatic Falcons'.**

When the pigeons get fed up with the scenery at Trafalgar Square, just up the road, or the quantity and quality of their food has taken a nosedive due to lack of tourists, they take great delight in moving home and coming to irritate us instead. And believe me, are they irritating! You take your life in your hand dashing across the Quadrangle to avoid getting splattered. All our window ledges have wire strung across them to prevent birds perching there and damaging and defacing the walls of our Grade I Listed building, but it takes our falcons to really convince them that they are definitely *not* wanted. They usually get the message.

I'm not sure whether The Treasury over the road has their own falcons. Their building is listed also. If so, they probably have only one as it's cheaper, and as befits their less illustrious Government Department than ours!

Which brings me back to looking after the fabric of our historic, unique and very beautiful Office. Very costly, but well worth it (to the Treasury's chagrin, I expect). The higher up you went in the building, the less elegant it became: our offices were adequate and functional, but save for the odd antique fireplace here and there, they were nothing special. However, we often had lovely views over Whitehall, and I became very attached to my own office on the third floor overlooking Horse Guards Parade when I came back from Hungary and was working for the Head of Western European Department. Mind you, listening to umpteen rehearsals for Trooping of the Colour became something of a distraction when I was trying to concentrate or speak on the phone! But I loved it nevertheless.

I never failed to be so immensely proud of where I worked. I was on a home posting from Mexico when the major refurbishment of the Foreign Office took place between 1986 and 1994. It was difficult at times working with all the mess, but the transformation was remarkable and so many hidden gems came to light, which were a joy to look at. Unknown paintings were revealed beneath other ones, and the cleaning of those already there brought a new vibrancy to the beautiful public areas. It was painstaking work carried out by experts, and they purposely left some bits of the old paint and paper on the walls just to show how dirty and grimy everywhere had become over the decades. The result, however, was reward enough for visiting dignitaries and those of us who worked there.

You used to be able to do the 'String of Pearls' tour, of all the historic buildings in which various Government Departments were housed (yes, even the Treasury). I don't know if this happens these days, especially after Covid, but if you ever do get the opportunity to look over the Foreign Office, it is definitely worth it. However, do beware of the pigeons!

Chapter Three

Embassies and High Commissions

As soon as I joined the Diplomatic Service, I had to learn about Embassies and High Commissions. I had to make sure I was *au fait* with what an Embassy actually does, and the difference between a High Commission and an Embassy. The former, headed by a High Commissioner, is the Embassy equivalent in countries of the Commonwealth.

To help to understand Embassy life, an Embassy is headed by the Ambassador, and then a Minister or Head of Chancery (H of C) or both, depending on the size of the Mission.
There are six sections in a British Embassy.

Chancery
Under the Head of Chancery (H of C), this is the political section and is concerned with increasing Britain's influence abroad and putting over the government of the day's foreign policies.

Commercial Section
Their aim is to promote British industry abroad, assist British companies in gaining commercial contracts, become involved in trade fairs, and work with the British Chamber of Commerce.

Consulates and the Consular Section
This is, perhaps, the best-known section as its aim is to protect and help British subjects abroad, make prison visits, identify and repatriate bodies, and issue visas. This is always a very busy department, especially in tourist hot-spots.

To date there are eight **Consulates General**, as opposed to Embassies or High Commissions, headed by a Consul General. In some cases, as in

Guatemala, where I was posted in 1981, when Britain breaks off diplomatic relations with that country, our Embassy is downgraded to a Consulate General.

We also have many **Consulates** around the world, mainly in the larger countries. The difference between an Embassy and a Consulate is that the former is the principal representative office of the home country, whereas a Consulate is an additional office offering facilities for the issue of passports, registration of births, and many other services for subjects of the home country.

Embassies, Consulates-General and Consulates are all considered legal territory of the home country, and as such the host country has no jurisdiction over them and cannot enter them. They are our 'fortress' in times of unrest, for which we are immensely grateful.

In addition to all these, there are also numerous Honorary Consuls in various large cities or remote areas around the world. Their role is to assist British subjects should they get into difficulties, and act as a link between that region and the Embassy/High Commission in the capital. They are normally prominent businessmen who perform their work on an honorary basis and are not paid a fee for their services. They have Diplomatic Passports, and diplomatic immunity.

I always felt, and still do, that the Foreign Office often gets a bad press when dealing with British Subjects abroad, and that expectations of what we can actually do are unrealistic. We are *not* the "Bank of FCO" as some believe!

Administration Section

Depending on whether Admin would listen to your pleas for new furniture, a new cooker, or whatever else you required, you either loved or hated this Section in equal measure at different times. It dealt with all the problems associated with a Mission: accommodation, furnishings, customs clearances for baggage and cars; medical problems; servants; leave arrangements etc. It was always very busy and, under a UK based Head, had an invaluable team of locally employed personnel to help navigate the usually unfathomable local customs. There was always a local "Mr. Fix It" who often got complaints when things didn't go too well, but rarely compliments when they did.

Information Section
Their aim is to promote Britain abroad and to aid and encourage tourism to our shores.

Defence Section
An important part of an Embassy, Defence Section is involved in the procurement of defence contracts, advising and training foreign military personnel, and putting forward HMG's defence policies.

In larger posts, like Washington and Paris, all three Services are represented, but in smaller Missions there is a Defence Attaché whose post is rotated amongst the Army, Navy and Air Force. There is also an Assistant Defence Attaché whose rank depends on the grade of the Embassy. This Section, too, is much involved in Royal Navy ship visits, and those of senior military personnel from either the UK or the host country, who are on official business.

Safety and security are of prime importance to us abroad, of course, and for that reason, depending on size and location, each Mission has at least one **Security Officer**, usually a retired member of the police or military. They are essential, and we are so grateful for the work they do in protecting us and keeping us safe.

The Queen's Messengers (QMs) - 'The Silver Greyhound'
The emblem of the Queen's (now King's) Messengers is a silver greyhound. During Charles 11's exile, he appointed four trusted men to carry messages to Royalist troops in England, and as a sign of their authority, he broke off four silver greyhounds from a bowl familiar to royal courtiers, and gave one to each man. From that date, the silver greyhound has become the symbol of the Corps of Queen's [King's] Messengers.

Just to explain further. The safe passage of Diplomatic Baggage is guaranteed by the Vienna Convention. The Bag is closed by a special seal and has its own passport. It cannot be X- rayed, opened or weighed, nor does it go in the hold: it must remain with the QM in the passenger cabin at all times.

The British Council.
This is a separate, but again important, part of the Foreign Office whose job it is to promote British culture and artists abroad, advise on education and provide English teachers. The Council doesn't always have an easy time, particularly in Communist countries or countries with repressive régimes, but it does vital work and is a lifeline to some of the world's poorer communities.

The Locally Employed.
And, finally, but by no means least, no Embassy, High Commission or British Council could function without that loyal, dedicated, and patient group of people, the locally employed. In my time a few of them were ex-pats, but mainly they were nationals of the country in which we were living. They worked tirelessly on our behalf in every department (because of the political/secret nature of our work, Chancery was the only area of the Embassy to which they had no access), and I know we were all so grateful for their advice and support. We didn't mix socially very much: they had their lives and we had ours. But they became our (and my) friends and I cannot speak highly enough of them.

The Diplomatic Service Wives Association (DSWA)
(Now The Diplomatic Service Families Association)

Times have changed since I was in The Office, and now there are quite a few spouses/partners at Post. I am sure they still carry out the same functions and offer the same help as the wives did, although quite a few work these days, which was not always possible when I was working in the Embassies abroad.

It cannot have been easy being a "Dippy Wife" (no disrespect intended: that was just what we called them). They contributed greatly (unpaid) to helping their husband's career and the number of dinner parties and receptions they gave was admirable. Having to send your young children off to boarding school must also be so hard for both husband and wife.

The wives also got involved in local projects, including, in Manila, secretly helping to run a "centre" at the Anglican church in Forbes Park to educate Filipina women on contraception.

The DSWA were (and still are, I imagine) also instrumental in helping to compile our very comprehensive **Post Reports**, booklets about a post given to us before we left to take up our assignment, and which we had to return before we left London. These are sensitive documents, and include, amongst other things: a brief resumé of the political situation; personal security advice; local customs and sensibilities; employing staff; where to shop and what was available to buy. I always found them extremely useful.

But it was at Post that the members of the DSWA were invaluable. During my time in The Office, the wives were responsible for running the **Commissary**, where we could buy necessary items that were not available in the local shops, for example certain foods, wine, make-up. There were set times when 'the shop' was open and there was always a queue.

Another important part of the DSWA role was looking after the *float* at Post. These were the emergency household items that were meant to tide us over until our baggage arrived. It was, of necessity, very basic, especially if there were a few new members of the Embassy arriving at once. For us singles, it usually comprised of a change of bedlinen, a blanket, two pillows, three towels, not much cutlery, two saucepans, one frying pan and kettle. If we were really desperate for something, the wives would try to find it or, if they could not, we would try to borrow it until our own baggage turned up. I was always grateful for the *float*, and found I could usually exist for a few weeks, but when it became months, as in Mexico, then things got a bit more difficult, and the wives did what they could to help.

I always had the utmost admiration for the wives and counted them among my good friends at the Embassy, even though their lives were very different to mine.

PART THREE

On Her Majesty's Diplomatic Service
1976 - 2005

Chapter Four

The New Civil Servant

My Appointment

And so here I was at last, a member of that most prestigious of Government Departments, the Foreign & Commonwealth Office. Shoulders back. I'm more than ready. After three years with P&O as an Assistant Purser, having braved numerous typhoons and hurricanes, I can handle anything, I told myself, and I prayed fervently that I could. Little did I know then how tested I would be!

I've come to the conclusion that my life has been one long abbreviation or acronym! It was bad enough with P&O. Now, with the FCO, it was about to get much worse.

My comprehensive letter of appointment arrived on 8 June 1976, as you can see. The letter is self-explanatory, so I won't go into too much detail about the Conditions of Service but will add my own comments.

I reported for duty as requested, and met Miss Lofting, a slightly formidable lady when you first met her, but very kind and caring, as I was to find out later. She sat me down and we went through my employment and what would be expected of me. I was already overqualified with eight 'O" Levels and three 'A' levels (French, Spanish and History) instead of the requisite five 'O's; and I met all the other criteria. I was single; over the minimum joining age of twenty-one-("you're rather old to be joining us at thirty-one" she said); and had the necessary 120 wpm Pitman's Shorthand and 70 wpm typing. More importantly, I spoke French and Spanish, which was a real bonus for The Office.

My letter of appointment to HM Diplomatic Service, which I was so proud to receive. Written on pale blue notepaper used only by Ambassadors and for important official correspondence .

Foreign and Commonwealth Office

London SW1A 2AH

8 June 1976

Miss G L Angrave
9 The Crossway
Loansdean
Morpeth
Northumberland

Dear Miss Angrave

     I am pleased to tell you that you have been appointed on a probationary basis to be a member of the Secretarial Branch (Grade US3) in Her Majesty's Diplomatic Service on the following terms:

1.   The appointment will date from 5 July 1976 and will carry a basic starting salary (including London Weighting) of £2162 per annum in the scale £2162 to £2579. Your incremental date will be 5 July. As already explained, arrangements will be made for you to take a tabulation typing test within a few days of joining, on the successful completion of which you will be appointed an S2, the salary scale (including London Weighting) being £2495 to £3125 per annum, and your incremental date will be changed accordingly. In addition to the salary figures for both Grades, a Supplement to Pay of £313.20 per annum is payable. When you have successfully completed your probationary period of 3 years your appointment will be confirmed.

2.   You should attend for duty at 11am on Monday 5 July reporting to me at room 315 Curtis Green Building, Victoria Embankment, London SW1A 2JD. You should bring with you parts 2 and 3 of your income tax form P45 which you should obtain from your previous employer.

3.   The enclosed questionnaire should be completed and returned in the official paid envelope addressed to Mr Eates, Security Department as soon as possible. This procedure is part of the security measures adopted by Her Majesty's Government for examining the records of persons in the public service whose work may be of particular secrecy and your appointment is subject to the satisfactory outcome of these enquiries. Would you also please send your birth certificate in the enclosed envelope addressed to Miss P A Mattocks of this Department. This is required for establishment purposes and will be returned to you in due course.

/4.

4.   Your main conditions of service at present are given below
and in Diplomatic Service Regulations, a copy of which will be
handed to you within two weeks of your appointment.   You will
also find much useful information about conditions of service
generally in the 'Handbook for the New Civil Servant'.   Any
significant changes in these conditions will be notified by
means of Office Circulars.

5.   OFFICIAL SECRETS

You will be bound by the provisions of the Official Secrets
Acts.

6.   HOURS

While in London you will normally work a 5 day week of 41 hours
including meal breaks.   Overtime or time off in lieu will be
granted for any additional hours worked.   There is no standard
working week for members of the Diplomatic Service overseas and
no overtime is payable.

7.   LEAVE

In addition to the public holidays and privilege holidays, which
total 9½ days in London, your annual leave allowance is 18 days.
On appointment as an S2 your annual leave allowance will be
increased, making a total of 20 days.   Annual leave allowances
applicable overseas are set out in Diplomatic Service
Regulations.

8.   SICK LEAVE

There is provision for granting sick leave with pay;   details
are given in Diplomatic Service Regulations.

9.   NATIONAL INSURANCE

National Insurance contributions will be deducted from your
salary and you will be liable for compulsory contributions under
the Social Security Act of 1973.

10.   SUPERANNUATION

Superannuation benefits are provided under the principal Civil
Service Pension Scheme, which is non contributory.

/11.

11. NOTICE

Unless you are dismissed on disciplinary grounds and provided you have served continuously for 13 weeks or more, the following minimum periods of notice will normally apply:

    (a) Less than 10 years service, 5 weeks

    (b) More than 10 years continuous service, 9 weeks

12. GRIEVANCES

If you have any grievances relating to your employment, you should first approach your immediate superior or, where this would be inappropriate, your Head of Department, Head of Chancery or Head of Post. The initial approach should be made informally; thereafter a written statement of grievance may be submitted. Should you still feel dissatisfied, you may bring your grievance to the notice of the Head of the appropriate Department of the Administration, but you should keep the person to whom you first expressed your grievance informed of the action you are taking. If you consider that the cause for complaint has not been dealt with satisfactorily in spite of these approaches, you may submit your complaint direct to the Chief Clerk who will, if necessary, refer the matter to the Head of the Diplomatic Service or to the Secretary of State. Additionally you are free to raise the matter with your Staff Association who may take action on your behalf. This procedure does not, of course preclude an officer who wishes to make a complaint on a personal matter affecting her position in the Service from bringing this directly and in confidence to the attention of a visiting Inspector or the Head of the appropriate Department in the Administration.

13. STAFF ASSOCIATION MEMBERSHIP

You are strongly encouraged to join the appropriate Staff Association, but under the Industrial Relations Act, you have the right to choose whether or not you do so. Nevertheless, the Administration regard it as being very much in the individual's own interests to belong to a Staff Association which can support her in her reasonable claims and represent her point of view on all kinds of questions affecting her welfare and her terms and conditions of service.

Yours sincerely

I. Lofting

Miss I Lofting
Personnel Operations Department

However, I was still placed on a three-year probationary period like every new entrant and was required to take a very difficult typing tabulation test within days of starting, which I had to pass. I then became an S2 (Secretary 2), and when I had successfully completed the three years, my appointment would be confirmed. After ten years, I would become an S1, that is a Senior PA, with the commensurate increase in pay.

It was explained to me in more detail than in the letter that, as a PA, I wouldn't be a Diplomat *per se,* but a member of the Secretarial Cadre (ie support staff). There were differences: grades of pay, pensions, rent allowance for our accommodation, the sort of car we could buy (in some countries we were given CD registration plates as in Hungary, whilst in others, like the Philippines, PAT plates denoting we were members of the Embassy but not Diplomats).

This was fine when I first started, but as the years rolled by it became a bone of contention for my PA colleagues and myself. Why were we not Diplomats too? We had the highest security clearance; our work by its very nature was secretive, sensitive, and socially delicate. We knew far more about what was going on than some of the Diplomats in other Sections. Fair enough, we could progress no further than S1 unless we wished to change over to the Diplomatic side, but this depended on how long we had served and whether The Office thought we were worthy of this change in status. I was asked fairly often if I would like to change, but it would have meant starting at the bottom as a junior Grade 9 in jobs that were nowhere near as interesting as being Ambassador's PA, so I declined. I was lucky with my colleagues in my postings, but there was the odd occasion when we felt like 'us' and 'them', and that we PAs were somehow less important than the Diplomats. Fortunately, not often, but it still rankled somewhat. And as PAs, we were expected to work all hours God sends (my words, not theirs), and we did!

The Official Secrets Act

Once Miss Lofting had explained all this, the very first thing I had to do was to sign the Official Secrets Act which binds me to secrecy to this day about certain aspects of my work. We went through the provisions in greater detail, and this I did. As a Senior PA in particular, I would be handling documents and information of the highest classification, so it was of paramount importance that I could be trusted.

Official Secrets Acts

Declaration To be signed by members of Government Departments on appointment and, where desirable, by non-civil servants on first being given access to Government information.

My attention has been drawn to the provisions of the Official Secrets Acts set out on the back of this document and I am fully aware of the serious consequences which may follow any breach of those provisions.

I understand that the sections of the Official Secrets Acts set out on the back of this document cover material published in a speech, lecture, or radio or television broadcast, or in the Press or in book form. I am aware that I should not divulge any information gained by me as a result of my appointment to any unauthorised person, either orally or in writing, without the previous official sanction in writing of the Department appointing me, to which written application should be made and two copies of the proposed publication be forwarded. I understand also that I am liable to be prosecuted if I publish without official sanction any information I may acquire in the course of my tenure of an official appointment (unless it has already officially been made public) or retain without official sanction any sketch, plan, model, article, note or official documents which are no longer needed for my official duties, and that these provisions apply not only during the period of my appointment but also after my appointment has ceased. I also understand that I must surrender any documents, etc., referred to in section 2 (1) of the Act if I am transferred from one post to another, save such as have been issued to me for my personal retention.

Signed *Gillian L. Angrave*

Surname (*Block letters*) ANGRAVE

Forename(s) GILLIAN LINDA

Date 5TH JULY 1976

E 74

Positive Vetting

This heralded the start of my Positive Vetting procedure, the outcome of which depended on whether or not I could continue with this employment. Such checks on my loyalty and suitability were essential, and if I did not satisfy the very strict security requirements of Her Majesty's Government, I could not proceed.

I completed the lengthy questionnaire, as requested, and returned it to the Security Department. This was then rigorously investigated. All the people whom I had listed as contacts - friends, family - were then either visited personally (as were Mum and Dad), even if it meant going abroad to do so, or contacted by telephone by the Security Officer specifically assigned to me (always a man in my case). They were asked in-depth personal questions about me, though I never knew anything about this as they were asked never to disclose what had been said. I also sent my Birth Certificate to Miss Mattocks in POD.

These "checks" were on-going throughout my whole career, and every five years or so I had to return home for an in-depth briefing and questioning by my officer. I never particularly looked forward to these interviews as they covered every aspect of my life, including romantic relationships, but I understood they were very necessary. "I'm not here to judge you, Gillian", he would say. "Just to ascertain the facts". Fine by me. There were one or two slightly embarrassing moments, but he was always satisfied, and I passed the test.

As stated, my basic starting salary per annum (including London Weighting which was paid because it was more expensive to live in London than elsewhere) was £2,162.00, rising to £2,495.00 after I had passed the dreaded tabulation test. A Supplement to Pay of £313.00 pa was also payable for my secretarial qualifications. Later I would receive a language allowance for my Spanish and French. This depended on being posted to a Spanish- or French-speaking country: if I was not, my allowance was reduced. However, there weren't too many PAs with my linguistic abilities, so I was fortunate enough to be posted mostly to Spanish-speaking countries, earning me the full allowance of about £500 p.a.

But to gain this extra amount, it was also a requirement that every five years I had to re-sit the Institute of Linguists exam in both languages. I always qualified at Intermediate level, never quite being able to pass at Advanced Level, which was really for interpreters. But I was happy with this, and to this day still enjoy my weekly U3A Spanish conversation groups.

It was also recommended that I join the PCSA (Public and Civil Service Association), a forerunner to UNISON: just in case!

A Member of the Diplomatic Service at Last
I was elated when everything had been checked and verified and I received confirmation of my employment at last. I learned that each officer had their own Personnel Officer dealing with that particular grade (mine was Miss Lofting). These Personnel Officers helped with career progression, advised on Selection Boards and helped with settling in once you were back on a Home Posting.

I also found that there was a separate **Travel Section** (indispensable) dealing with postings abroad: obtaining the necessary visa clearance; health issues, including getting the requisite vaccinations; security training; airline bookings; packing up of heavy baggage, Unaccompanied Air Freight, etc. The list was endless and I for one relied on them a lot.

I gather that today all this is left to the individual officer working mainly on-line, searching, and applying for postings, making one's own travel bookings, packing, and sorting out health requirements. A time consuming and onerous task, but that's progress.

However, there are compensations. The Office has become more 'user-friendly'. Conditions abroad are better (more leave, breather journeys when at difficult posts, and more choice of destinations); more family-friendly policies, i.e. job-sharing; and SUPL (Supernumerary Unpaid Leave) whereby a person can take five years unpaid leave to bring up a family, though you might lose out on promotion prospects to a slight degree.

But all my ex-FCO friends and colleagues agree that we had the best years, when the number of people working for the FCO was far fewer and we were all one big, close family. I wouldn't have had it any other way.

Cypher Duties

Once I had received my confirmation, one of the additional duties I would be expected to fulfil when on a posting was that of Duty Officer/Cypher Clerk. Depending on the Mission, this happened every four weeks or so. For that reason, it was vital that I learned how to operate the current cypher machine. When I joined, The Office had just progressed from the slow and tedious Book Cypher decoding method to something that was heralded as the best thing since sliced bread by the Communications (Comms) Department - *Noreen*! Really?

My best friend, NOREEN
©Crown Copyright, by kind permission Director, GCHQ

I have just enquired of the GCHQ Museum Curator where the name *Noreen* comes from. He said the machine's real title is BID/590 (just the basic one-up numbering system), but they are given nicknames at the time, by whom it is uncertain. I presume the person concerned with labelling this machine was familiar with a temperamental female of that name. She certainly was that!

Bless her cotton socks! I can disclose now, as she has taken up residence in the GCHQ Museum, making me feel extremely old, that this was a 'contraption' working with Murray Code tape, that is holes punched into the tape signifying each letter. The keyboard was similar, but not quite the same, as a manual typewriter (which is the only typewriter we used for our PA work in those days), so once I got used to her, I could type as fast as she would allow, which was very slow as it took a lot of pressure to press the keys! It was tiring, laborious work, which needed great concentration, and heaven help you if you broke the tape. Trying to find out where you were was a nightmare. I've described this again in my Falklands Chapter, to give you some idea of what could go wrong.

In time, we gravitated to *Alvis* (I wonder who he was?), which did away with the tapes and was more like a telex machine. Then on to *Topic*, like a very basic computer. But to begin with, I was stuck with *Noreen*.

So, to familiarize myself with this 'lady', I spent many a happy hour in a noisy room above the Passport Office in Petty France, near St James's tube station, learning all about her little foibles. And did she have some! I used to go cross-eyed at times, but it had to be done and I was tested on it afterwards. Fortunately, I passed with flying colours, which is just as well as I had to use her often throughout my career.

Health

Ever felt like a pin cushion? I did. During my Foreign Office years, most of my postings were in Third World countries, where we had our own (local) Embassy doctors and dentists who were constantly monitored by our Department of Health, and a list of hospitals (private) to which we would go if necessary. Hygiene standards were not always of the highest in these countries, and, inevitably, I succumbed to quite a few "afflictions, but I survived.

Therefore, before I could go abroad, I had to have almost every vaccination known to man, so it seemed: Yellow Fever, typhoid, cholera, rabies, Hepatitis A and B, polio, tuberculosis, diphtheria and (thank you Hungary) ticks! I've still got most of my certificates. Tony Hancock might have had an empty left arm: I had a full one! (You need to be of a certain age to understand that comment.)

And so now, after satisfying all the requirements to become a member of the Diplomatic Service, I looked forward eagerly to my future itinerant life.

But first I had to have a spell in The Office and was sent to work as PA to Humphrey Maud, Head of Financial Relations Department (Heads of Department were Ambassadors or High Commissioners when abroad). He was extremely nice and, whilst the work itself was not the most interesting, I enjoyed it.

My First Posting

Normally you can reckon on spending at least a few months, if not longer, in London before going abroad. But after six weeks I got a call from Miss Lofting asking me to go and see her as she had a posting for me. Gosh, I thought, this can't be bad. There's a definite advantage to being an old entrant! So off I went, excited to know what she had in mind.

"We'd like you to go to Antigua for two and a half years, Gillian," she said.

My heart sank. Oh no. Not Antigua. I'd been there so many times before with P&O, and whilst it was very pleasant and I had enjoyed my visits, the thought of being stuck in St John's for so long did not fill me with glee. I said so to a horrified Miss Lofting. One **never** turned down a posting, but here was a new entrant who did! So I returned, dejected, to FRD and thought "That's done it. Now I'll be here for years."

But not so. I received another call about two weeks later, offering me Manila for three years, working as PA to the Counsellor/Consul General/Chargé, Peter George. I was overjoyed, much to an astounded Miss Lofting, who probably thought that sending me to a Third World country instead of an idyllic Caribbean Island would teach me not to refuse in future. Sorry to disappoint! However, she was not to know that I loved the Far East and South-East Asia, having been there often too. I thanked her profusely; she said she was pleased I would like to go; and so the wheels were set in motion for me to leave London in October. I was on the move again at last.

Travel Section

I never realized just how much there was to do before a posting. I was in daily touch with Travel Section, who were wonderful. The Post Report dropped into my in-tray, along with numerous memos about vaccination appointments, dates for packers, arrangement of a car loan to buy my British Escort. Remember, there were no computers or emails in those days. I had a long to-do list, which gradually got smaller, until finally the day arrived for me to fly to Manila.

I was so excited, but so sad at the same time as this meant leaving dear Mum and Dad yet again. They were genuinely pleased for me and proud that I had found such a prestigious job, and they hastily poured over the map to see just exactly where the Philippines were.

"Gillian's going to the Philistines", my Auntie Gladys announced to all and sundry. "No, not Philistines, Gladys, Philippines", Mum corrected.

And so, armed with a new passport, a plethora of vaccination certificates, and enough information to turn my little grey cells even greyer, I girded my loins and set off in floods of tears (Mum and Dad too) from Birmingham, where I had been staying with them for those last few days, down to Heathrow to catch my flight to New Delhi where I was stopping over (as was allowed) for four days, before travelling to Singapore for two nights, and then finally on to Manila.

I was ready now to take on the Philistines, who proved to be anything but!

PART FOUR

From Office to Home

Chapter Five

My Embassies

As you will have gathered by now (I think), I'm a methodical and organized soul, and so I shall take each Embassy in the order to which I was posted there. I'll also give a brief account of how I arrived and left Post, though there's only one truly memorable journey. My grateful thanks go to Mark Bertram, who was Head of Overseas Estates Department (OED), based in Croydon, during my time in The Office. Mark has written 'Room for Diplomacy' (his website is www.roomfordiplomacy.com) which gives a detailed history and the specifications of our properties abroad, and has provided much of the information to help me with this Chapter and the next. Apart from the historical photographs, again Mark's, the rest are my own. So here goes!

THE PHILIPPINES

Electra House, Legazpi Village, Makati, Manila

When I arrived in Manila and saw the Embassy for the first time, to say that I was somewhat underwhelmed was an understatement. It was not what I had expected an Embassy to look like – the sixth floor of an office block. I imagined an elegant mansion, as in Paris. Just shows how wrong a new entrant can be! Previously the Embassy had occupied leased premises near to the Residence in Roxas Boulevard, but it moved in 1975 to the Ionian Building, later called Electra House, at 115-7 Esteban Street (they moved again in 1989).

The building was in the centre of Legazpi Village, an up-and-coming commercial area in the suburb of Makati. It was a bit of a building site still, and if I remember correctly, we parked our cars on the waste ground opposite. But it was near to where we all lived, which was far more practical and accessible than downtown Manila. I had a nice office of my own next to my boss Peter's, and the rest of the layout was functional and adequate, though we did seem to be a bit squashed at times. We didn't mix with the other tenants in the block: I think my only contact was with the janitor, whom I had cause to wake up a few times in the middle of the night when I was on duty and needed access.

To and From Post

Depending on the distance from London, we were allowed time (taken out of our leave) to get to a Post. We always flew British Airways where possible, and Club Class on journeys of more than two and a half hours duration. Otherwise, it was Economy. The Ambassador always flew First Class.

The one good thing about being sent to the Philippines was that there was a wide choice of destinations you could stop off at *en route*, and because of the distance from London, Manila qualified for mid-tour leave after eighteen months. On my initial journey out, Richard Thomas, the new Head of Financial Relations Department where I was working at the time, kindly arranged for me to stay with a colleague in New Delhi for four days. I didn't know this lady at all, but The Office was like one big happy family and colleagues were usually pleased to put you up for a day or so, if convenient. It was an interesting stay in India, (though I suffered from *Delhi Belly* part of the time) and I managed to visit the Taj Mahal, Fatehpur Sikri, the Red Fort, the Qutub Minaret – anywhere within a day's reach of New Delhi. I was glad to have had the opportunity to stop off there, but it reinforced my feeling that I never wanted to be posted to the Sub-Continent. It just wasn't for me.

The British High Commission New Delhi

From New Delhi, I continued to Singapore for two nights. I'd visited this alluring city many times before with P&O on-board CANBERRA and ORIANA, so I was anxious to see how it had changed, if at all. Sadly (to me), it had. The city had become more sanitized. Boogie Street and Change Alley had lost a lot of their character, and even part of the luxurious gardens of the Raffles Hotel had been sacrificed for a new main road, such is progress. I then journeyed on to Manila.

Eighteen months soon passed, and I was due my month's mid-tour leave. On board CANBERRA, I had become very good friends with Herb and Janee Dimmitt. Herb was Vice President of the big department store J C Penney in Honolulu, and they were passengers with us *en route* to Sydney, where they were spending a few weeks. We hadn't had the best of beginnings as I told them they wouldn't be allowed to land anywhere in Australia as they had no visas. They were not pleased, but I said I would accompany them to the Australian Consulate in Suva where they could obtain the relevant entry permits, which I did. After that, as I said, we became the best of friends, and I stayed in constant touch with them wherever I went.

They knew I was in Manila and was going home on mid-tour leave, so they kindly invited me to stay a week with them on my way back to the UK. They lived in the most amazing house on Diamond Head, with a large swimming pool, overlooking Honolulu and the ocean. It was idyllic. Herb and I played golf, and as a surprise, they took me on a flight to Maui to stay at their luxurious condominium on that island. Again, perfect. I never forgot that holiday, and we talked about it a lot afterwards. Sadly, they died quite a few years ago now, but I still miss them.

However, I had to continue my journey and be home in time for my sister Sheila's wedding. I was to be her Matron of Honour and I wouldn't have missed it for the world.

When my month was up, I headed back to Manila via Sri Lanka for three days: again fascinating, but not for me.

When I finally left Manila at the end of my tour, I treated myself to a BA Stop-Over Holiday at The Reef Hotel in the Seychelles for five days. Luxury personified. My room was right on the beach, and I took taxis to Victoria, and out and about as much as I could, including an interesting trip to a beach to spend time with giant turtles. I even managed a round of golf – but more about that under '**Sport**'.

PERU

When I arrived at Lima, I was faced with yet another office block at Plaza Washington. Where were all these imposing Embassy buildings? We had bought the 12th and 13th floors of the *Edificio República* in Plaza Washington in 1974.   It was fine being high up

Our Embassy building (12th and 13th floors) in Plaza Washington, Lima

when the lift was working, not quite so fine when it wasn't. However, you did get spectacular views of Lima and, in the distance, the Andes, when you had the time to look out of the window and it wasn't the 'smog season' (May to October), when you rarely saw the sun at all. We parked our cars in front, and you can just see my little orange VW Beetle to the left.

The Embassy remained there until 2002, when it moved to *Torre Parque Mar*, Avenida José Larco, Miraflores, just round the corner from where my flat was. This would have been ideal and saved me a hair-raising journey each morning down the 'Grand Prix' ring road to Plaza Washington, but in my time there, it was not to be.

To and From Post

There were no BA flights to Lima in those days. I had to fly either to Schipol and then join a KLM flight to Lima, or I could fly BA to Miami and then onwards on AeroPeru. I chose the former, and I will never forget my first sight of Lima. It was like looking down on a white glove. All the valleys were shrouded in mist up to the foothills of the snow-capped Andes towering above them. And away from the city, the desert stretched along the coast into the distance, both to the north and south, like a strand of gold thread beneath the mountains. It was so beautiful.

My journey leaving Peru was fraught, as you will gather further on.

GUATEMALA

Things were not much better when I got to Guatemala, but at least this was an hotel and not an office block! Because of the civil war raging in that country, and the tensions between the UK and Guatemala over Belize, our Consulate-General was then

The British Consulate General, Suite 5,
Hotel El Conquistador, Via 5, Guatemala City

housed in the fifth floor suite of the *Hotel El Conquistador*, not too far from the downtown area of Guatemala City. This was not ideal, of course, but we were due to move into a new Consulate-General building in October (1981), so we managed as best we could. At least the food the hotel sent up to us was good! I gather that the Embassy today is housed in the swish new glass fronted *Edificio Torre Internacional*, in the modern suburb of Zona 10.

On 11 September 1981, the day of our expulsion from the country, the new Consulate-General was bombed, and all the windows were blown out. I don't know what subsequently happened to that building, but it wasn't until 1994 that we resumed diplomatic relations with Guatemala.

To and From Post

The only way to get to Guatemala from Lima was to fly up to Miami and then down again. This suited me fine, as it gave me the chance to stay for two nights with my good friend, Pat, who had settled there before I went to sea and married an American. It was good to see her again, and I needed the respite after my time in Lima.

Leaving Guatemala, I had no choice. We UK based spent three nights in Miami after our traumatic expulsion, and then caught the night BA flight back to London, to safety and security at last.

CHILE

I was beginning to think I was destined not to work in a grand Embassy building. In Santiago we occupied yet another unremarkable office block in Avenida La Concepción, in the residential suburb of Providencia. Formerly, the Embassy had been in small buildings in the grounds of the Residence at 152 Avenida Vicuña Mackenna. In 1951 it moved to the 3rd floor of the Bank of

The British Embassy, Avenida La Concepción, Santiago

London and South America at 1055 Calle Augustines. Then, by the time I arrived in Santiago in 1982, HMG had purchased (in 1974) the ground and top two floors of the five-storey building at 155 *Edificio La Concepción.* This was sold in 1992 and the Embassy moved yet again to its present site at 125 Avenida Bosque Norte, in the new commercial area of Las Condes.

Again, I took a direct KLM flight from Schipol to Santiago, not stopping anywhere. I was heading back to London for a home posting, and was intending to buy a flat, so I needed to be fairly abstemious – not that easy for me!

However, on leaving Chile on LAN Chile, I did treat myself to a stay for three nights in New Orleans on the way home. Dad and I were great trad jazz fans and I had promised him I would go to Preservation Hall to listen to the jazz there. It was fabulous, and Dad much enjoyed the cassette I brought back for him (no CDs available) and hearing over and over what it was like to be there. I'm so glad I went. Mum said that when Dad had Parkinsons, he still loved to listen to that music. It was one of the few things that he remembered, and it gave him endless pleasure until he died.

MEXICO

1987 - The Embassy, Río Lerma 71, Zona Rosa, Mexico City.
My office is over the porch.

The side of the Embassy, with the Consular Section back left.

At last! A building I deemed worthy of being called an Embassy.

Originally built to house the British legation (it became an Embassy in 1944), the land upon which the Embassy stood when I was there was purchased by a syndicate called The United States and Mexican Trust Company at the beginning of the 20th century and was named *The Cuauhtémoc Colony*. The Minister at the time, Reginald Tower, persisted (as they do) with his wish for a permanent house/legation to be built there. He was getting rather fed up as he was living in rented accommodation, the rent allowance was never enough, and he was always having to move. Eventually he succeeded (as they do), and HMG agreed to buy the freehold of a site at *Colonia Cuauhtémoc* belonging to a merchant called John Benjamin Body that had come up for sale in 1910 at a price of £7,746.

Then began the usual wrangling over the cost and style of a new house, until a design was finally approved by the Office of Works at a cost of about £16,500.

It remained the mission house and residence until 1950, when space became so cramped that the Residence moved out and it was converted to offices. A new wing was added in 1973 costing about £88,000, and an adjacent building was bought in 1980 for £27,000 to house the Consular Section, which had previously been located elsewhere in the DF since 1967.

I loved working there. My office had a single window over the front porch, with the Ambassador's impressive office having the two windows on the right.

It was a bit noisy, being on a busy street and nearly opposite the substantial American Embassy building, but that didn't matter as it was a great working environment, and couldn't have been in a better location, a short walk away from the fashionable restaurants and boutiques in the *Zona Rosa* (difficult to keep away - yet another 'financial disaster area'!). The Embassy grounds were impressive too, as was the separate Consular Section (to the left in the photograph). There was also a stunning staircase up to the first floor, where most of we UK based worked, with blue crafted Delft style tiles on the wall.

I gather that the two buildings were put on the market in May last year, 2021, and the Embassy has now moved to the 20th floor of a plush new office block, *Torre de Ángel*, on Paseo de la Reforma, Colonia Juaréz, not far away. I don't know whether there have been any takers for the site as yet. I would imagine so. Sad, though. I really liked our old Embassy.

Because of the dreadful congestion, overcrowding and pollution in Mexico City, where chest complaints were a regular occurrence, the Embassy also rented a guest house away from the DF, where we could stay for a day or so to get some respite. When I arrived, we had a very nice house at Yautepec, on the outskirts of Cuernavaca, to the south of the DF *en route* to Acapulco. I got to know this city fairly well during my time in Mexico, as it was where I spent my first month on an induction course, staying with a Mexican family. Although we had to book to give everyone a fair chance to stay at Yautepec, I went there fairly often, and even took some of the 'Licence to Kill' film crew there to give them a break from filming (more of that later).

Halfway through my tour, we gave up that property and rented another very nice house at Huastepec, to the west of the DF. For me the redeeming feature of this house was that it was on a golf course. I could play to my heart's content, and I did, walking onto the course from our garden in the evening, when few golfers were around, to practice on the 9th green and even manage the odd hole or two (sssh – don't tell anyone!).

Our Embassy guest houses: Yautepec and Huastepec

To and From Post

My journey out to Mexico was somewhat fraught. I was booked on a BA flight to Schipol, thence KLM to Mexico, on 17 October 1987, the day of Michael Fish's 'hurricane that never was' (he'll never live that down). All flights from the UK were cancelled: no-one was going anywhere. I missed my connection, and so I stayed with my best friend Pam, who worked for BA, and her Mum, who lived near Gatwick, until we could sort everything out. Eventually, I left Heathrow on 19 October and arrived at Mexico City on the 20th. I didn't stop over. I just wanted to get there.

I only had two weeks leave between Mexico and Hungary, and there was so much to do that I had to fly straight home. I would have liked to stop off somewhere, but there was no time.

HUNGARY

Yet another imposing building. Things were definitely looking up! Briefly, our former legation building was located in the Castle District of the hill town of Buda. This area was centred around the castle and Mátyás Church, 197 ft above the Danube, and is known today as *The Var*, now a very popular tourist area.

The British Embassy, Harminçad utca
Budapest (formerly the Hazai Bank)

The legation was both the home and office of the vice-consul, Carl Lutz, but it was destroyed and looted at the end of the Second World War. He had used it as a sanctuary for many of the thousands of Jews living in Hungary during that time. The building lay in ruins during the 1950s whilst HMG tried to decide what to do with the site, and it was eventually ceded to the Hungarian government in the mid-1960s. It was reconstructed and is now the Hungarian National Office of Cultural Heritage. A plaque dedicated to Carl Lutz was put on the wall by the main entrance in 2012.

At the end of the Second World War the Embassy needed to be located somewhere, so it rented space in the imposing Secessionist Hazai Bank building at Harminçad utca, Erzsébet tér.

The bank was built in 1914 and still operated as such during the following three decades. In 1944, after the German occupation of Hungary, the Bank played a vital role again in saving many Hungarian Jews by renting space to the Swedish consul, Raoul Wallenberg, who was there on a clandestine mission to help them. Wallenberg, because of his protected diplomatic status, declared his rented premises an official Swedish Consulate, not to be entered by Nazis, and he sheltered many Jews until his mysterious disappearance in 1945. No-one has ever found out what happened to him, nor where his remains lie. But a plaque is now on the wall commemorating his heroic deeds. We were very aware of this history when we worked there.

When our Embassy rented the whole of the building at the end of the War, it became a bastion of Western culture, much to the anger of the Communists when they invaded Hungary in 1956. I remember there were bullet holes in the outside walls. The Communists closely monitored all the comings and goings of visitors during the whole of the Cold War period, but when the Iron Curtain fell in 1989, we British celebrated by having the building completely renovated, the result of which is stunning. The marble staircase is truly beautiful. The work was completed in 1990, just in time for the visit of Prince Charles and Princess Diana; and I had the honour to be present when HM The Queen and HRH The Duke of Edinburg were in Budapest on a State Visit in May 1993 and Her Majesty inaugurated the newly renovated reception hall.

Much to my regret, we no longer have this beautiful building. When the lease expired in 2016, the Embassy moved over the River Danube to a two storey modern building in tree-lined Füge utca, in the Rózsadomb area of Buda. It looks like a very pleasant street and is close to where we all lived then (and still do I expect), but for me you can't beat the location of our old Embassy. It was near the Danube (not quite so ideal when the river flooded in July with snow melt) and close to the few shops there were in the pedestrianized Váçi ut.

But the most important thing of all: it was almost next door to the renowned patisserie, *Gerbeaud Cukrászda,* with its late 19th century décor, in Vörösmarty tér. Its history is fascinating: its frothy coffee, liqueurs and cream tortes, pure heaven! Needless to say, I used to pop in there often, with unwelcome consequences!

However, I never felt guilty. I still considered myself comparatively sylph-like in comparison with many of the Hungarian ladies, who were quite formidable and substantial at that time!

To and From Post

Of all my journeys to Post, the one to Hungary was the most memorable.

On learning I was going to Budapest, my first priority was to buy a car. Before I left Mexico, I applied for a car loan from The Office, to which they agreed. The Office would deposit the necessary funds into my bank account, and I would pay back an amount each month so that by the end of my tour I owed nothing (I had done this for all my cars).

As soon as I returned to the UK, I ordered a tax free, new design Escort 1.6 GLX (which was commensurate with my grade) from Dana Ford Forhandling A/S in Copenhagen, which offered the best deal. The only question was: how to get it from Denmark to Hungary? Answer: I would drive it there. This was far quicker than having it shipped, and cheaper for The Office. I was allowed travelling time, and someone could go with me for safety, so my best friend Pam eagerly said she would accompany me and act as navigator as, under the terms of my loan and insurance, only I was permitted to drive my diplomatic car.

My feet barely touched the ground during the short time I had back at home. The list of tasks got longer and longer: Mum and Dad to see, of course; new tenants to find for my flat; vaccinations to be brought up to date, and a new one for ticks to add to the collection. I was sent on a skid pan course at Thruxton to prepare me for the harsh Hungarian winters; and I had to do a day's computer training course as I had never used one, which reduced me to tears! Mouse? What mouse?

And of course, I had to work out how I was going to get to Budapest from Copenhagen. Pam and I mulled it over. I had hired a Hertz car for the time I was back in the UK. We would drive to Harwich; leave the car at the Hertz office there; catch the *Princess of Scandinavia* overnight ferry to Esbjerg; take the train to Copenhagen; two nights there to complete all the paperwork and pay the money; drive to Gröningen; one night there; two nights in the Bavarian town of Passau, on the German/Austrian border, to give us a break; a night in Vienna; then on to Budapest to arrive at the Embassy before lunch on 25th March. Simple! I set about making the bookings myself, though The Office would reimburse all our expenses. Jim Davis, a P&O Director and friend of Pam and me from our sea-going days, booked a nice cabin for us on the ferry (we even found a bottle of champagne waiting for us). So off we set on 18 March 1991, armed with enough maps to stock Stamfords, the famous travel bookshop near the Strand. No satnavs in those days. A small consideration – I also had 165 kgs of baggage to load into the cars somehow!

It was a rough crossing, but that didn't deter two ex-mariners like us. We arrived at Esbjerg at 1.15 pm, but it took so long to off-load my cases that we missed the train and I had to spend £100 to hire another car to drive us to Copenhagen. Neither of us had any idea of the route, but Pam's impressive navigating took us there safely and we wearily arrived in Copenhagen at 9 pm.

The next day, John Schroff, the Ford dealer, came to collect us from our hotel. It took all morning to complete the paperwork and transfer the money, after which John dropped us off near Stroget for some sightseeing. He came to collect us at 8.15 am the next morning to take us to the dealership, where I took delivery of my shiny new car, and Pam and I set off to catch the 12.10 pm ferry from Rodbyhavn to Puttingen. I could hardly see Pam for maps, but she has an excellent sense of direction (like me), so I knew I was in good hands. The weather was fine, and we arrived in the late afternoon at the comfortable *Hotel Rennschuh* at Gröningen.

Collecting the car in Copenhagen. Waiting to board
the ferry at Rodbyhavn

It was a long way to Passau. We set out early the next day in brilliant
sunshine, but the further south we drove the worse the weather
became until it was torrential rain. I'm used to left-hand drive cars,
but conditions on the autobahns were treacherous with all the spray.
We travelled all day and finally arrived at Passau at around 7 pm,
having spent ages driving round and round in circles through the
narrow streets trying to get to the *Hotel König* where we would be
staying. We knew where it was. We just couldn't get there!

The next day we had a well-earned, much needed rest. I managed
to find somewhere to get my hair cut, having not had time to do so
before I left the UK, and we spent the morning just wandering around
this beautiful city, also known as the *Dreiflüssestadt,* famous for its
baroque and gothic architecture, visiting the imposing St Stephen's
Church, which was a must. After that, we had a pleasant stroll
along the river walk and found a good restaurant for lunch. In
the afternoon, we took the informative Three Rivers boat tour,
Passau being at the confluence of the Rivers Danube, Inn and Ilz.

Off again the next day to the Austrian border. I presented the
relevant Customs documents, we sailed through with no problems,
and continued on to Vienna. There I had arranged for us to stay the

Passau

night at the flat of my good friends John and June Larden from my Manila days (John was now Security Officer in Vienna), who although they were away for a short break, had kindly said we could use their place. This meant collecting the keys from the Embassy and then finding their flat, but Pam's navigating was as brilliant as ever. By now it was mid-afternoon, which meant we had time to stretch our legs and do a bit of sightseeing. And, of course, we could not be in Vienna without tasting *sacher torte* (early training for Gerbeaud's?)

It was another early start the next day. We deposited the keys back at the Embassy, and headed for the Hungarian border, where we again encountered no problems, thankfully, though the Officers were amazed that we had driven all the way from Denmark on our own! One thing I hadn't appreciated when I bought my car, however, was just how difficult it was to get unleaded petrol in Eastern Europe. I learned fast, and always made sure I carried a full spare can wherever I went!

It's normally only two and a half hours to Budapest from the border (though I think it's quicker these days), so we were at the Embassy by midday. The Ambassador was away, returning late the next day, so Steve, the Admin Officer, briefly introduced me to some of my colleagues; we stocked up with groceries at the Commissary; and then followed him, on what seemed a really complicated route, to my new flat so that I could unpack and have a rest. We had a slight problem getting the gas stove to work, but finally managed to eat, and, having only the emergency *float* of equipment, spent a freezing night with only one blanket each. But we survived!

The next day, 26 March, Steve came to my flat early and I followed him to *The Var*, where I dropped Pam off so she could do yet more sightseeing, which she thoroughly enjoyed. I then followed him to the Embassy to meet my colleagues properly and start to settle in.

Pam arrived back at the Embassy at lunchtime and then she and I went with the driver and the Unclassified Diplomatic Bags to the airport. I was sad to wave her off: I was so grateful for her friendship and company, and it had certainly been a journey to remember. I couldn't have done it without her. Thanks, Pam.

Back then to the Embassy in readiness to start my new life in Hungary.

Arrived safe and sound! The British Embassy, Budapest, on 26th March 1991, with my blue Escort in the foreground

Subsequently, I was to drive on my own to and from the UK on a short spell of leave after The State Visit, and then back to the UK when I finally left Hungary.

These were long journeys, without the benefit of Pam's navigation, but I did it, though I was so tired when I arrived at my destination. I stayed both times at Passau (not at Vienna), which brought back happy memories, and from there my route took me via Regensburg, Nüremburg, Hockenheim, stopping the night near Bonn, and finally on to Zeebrugge to catch the ferry up to Hull. It was easier to go to Hull as I was staying with Mum and Dad near Shrewsbury. I did the journey in reverse when I went back to Hungary.

Knowing I was going back to the UK on a home posting, before I left Budapest I sold my faithful little Escort and bought a metallic red right-hand drive Rover from the newly opened dealership there. I stuffed it to the gunnels with suitcases, my TV, and as many other odds and ends as I could get in, but although I covered everything as best I could, I was always apprehensive about leaving the car anywhere overnight in case it got broken into.

I had a wonderful surprise when I reached Zeebrugge on my final trip. Out of habit, I looked at the list of Officers on the *Pride of Rotterdam* and saw, to my astonishment and delight, that the Purser was my old friend and shipmate, Mike Staddon. I hadn't seen him for twenty years, so I popped my head round his door. "Good God", he exclaimed. "It's Swilly Gilly" (nothing to do with drink, I promise you!). Although he was working, he took time out to have a quick cup of tea and we had as good a catch-up as we could. It was super to see him again, and now I'm retired I've seen him subsequently at our P&O Ancient Mariners' Reunions every year. We always have a laugh about that encounter.

Once in the UK, for Customs Duty purposes I had to keep the car for six months, after which time I sold it for (yes, you guessed it!) another Escort. I didn't know then that I wouldn't be going abroad again. But, thinking back, I've been so grateful for all the travelling I have done with The Office, both within and to and from the countries to which I was posted, and further afield. I've documented these 'wanderings' more in my Chapter on Travels, as there is much more to tell. One thing is certain, though. Wherever I have been, the memories and experiences of what I have seen and done will never leave me.

Back in the UK from Budapest.
This was to be my last foreign car.

Chapter Six

My Ambassadors' Residences

Of course, my Ambassadors had to live somewhere, and within the Overseas Estate that HMG owns, there are some truly magnificent Residences.

Again, my thanks go to Mark for all his help and advice on this Chapter.

THE PHILIPPINES

Our elegant Residence in Roxas
on the corner of Roxas Boulevard and del Pilar Street

This elegant, colonial style brick mansion on the corner of Roxas Boulevard and del Pilar Street in downtown Malate,, was purchased by HMG in 1946 for £44,000. It was war-damaged (hence the price), restored and partly rebuilt in 1948, and refurbished again in 1970 just before I went to Manila. To me, it epitomised HMG's standing in the Philippines. It was full of charm and character inside, and the tropical garden was beautiful. If I remember correctly, the wall stretched down to the sea front.

However, unfortunately there were two major drawbacks. The first was that now the Embassy had moved from the leased premises in Roxas Boulevard to another leased building in Makati, trying to reach the Residence from there on the crowded Manila streets was a nightmare. It took for ever and a day, and was completely impractical.

But there was a more pressing problem. The Residence was next door to a very high class brothel, the Pink Pussycat Club, which caused endless problems.

The rear of the Residence

One function stands out in particular. It was the occasion of the Queen's Birthday Party (QBP) at the beginning of June, 1975, when all of Manila's great and the good were invited. The 'ladies of the night' (and day!), on hearing what sounded like a really good party next door, climbed over the wall and starting mingling with the guests, touting for business. The Ambassador was horrified: so were most of the spouses and a few guests; but most of the men thought it highly amusing. However, this just wasn't the done thing at an official reception as important as the QBP. Our Security Officer had a really hard time evicting them, and the ladies then lined the front drive as the guests were leaving, still ever-hopeful of attracting some clients. Whether they did so or not, I don't know. But one thing was certain. Our QBP was the talk of the town for months to come, and everyone wanted an invite to a function at our Residence!

At the end of 1976, just after I arrived, it was decided that this situation could not continue, and the Residence was finally sold for £850,000.

Meanwhile, land had been purchased in 1973 for ££86,000 to build a new Residence (which then became 102 Cambridge Circle, North Forbes Park, Makati) and work started on the build. When Roxas Boulevard was sold, the Ambassador moved for a short time into rented accommodation, and finally occupied the new Residence in 1981 (it had cost about £500,000 to build). I don't have any photographs of the rented property, and nor do any of my friends, but from what I can remember it was a modern house, not very attractive, and lacking in atmosphere. However, it did have a swimming pool with a glass window, which was rarther disconcerting to think that people were looking at your legs as you were swimming along. And it was a bit odd to see these legs thrashing around if you were looking through the window, but interesting to see which legs belonged to whom! There were some cracking parties and receptions at this Residence, though, so it wasn't all bad. I didn't know the new Residence at all as I left Manila in 1980.

PERU

I don't have any photographs either of the Residence in Calle Atagupa, Huerta de San Antonio, Monterrico (an affluent suburb of Lima), which we purchased in 1972. Nor does Mark, nor any of my friends, I fear. It was an established property, with an adjacent smaller house, useful for guests. From what I can remember, it was pleasant looking, reasonably modern, with nice gardens which provided an elegant setting for receptions and other functions.

GUATEMALA

Our lives were very difficult in Guatemala, but the Residence was our saving grace. It was an elegant colonial style house, purchased freehold in 1947, occupying land for numbers 4-13, 7th Avenida, in the affluent residential area of Zona 9, not far from my own flat just off Avenida Reforma in Zona 10. I'm not sure whether we still have it today. I hope so.

The British Residence in Guatemala City in 1981

Because of the political situation and our problems over Belize, we had few visitors to the Consulate-General, so there was not a vast amount of entertaining being offered at the Residence, though Michael Wilmshurst, the Consul-General, and his wife Mary, did their best. At times I think we British were 'personae non gratae' – no-one wanted to be associated with us. But there were a few receptions, including the QBP which Michael was determined to host. Nothing quite so elaborate as Manila, nor memorable, but enjoyable nonetheless and appreciated by those few who came.

Three things I associate with the Residence. The first is *THE PARROT* (its real name escapes me – I only remember the one we gave it, which wasn't very complimentary!). When the Japanese Ambassador came to leave Guatemala, he didn't know exactly what to do with this lively bird, so he gave it to Michael as a present. I'm not sure Michael wanted it either, but out of the kindness of his heart, he took it in. Fine. I like birds (especially owls), but little did we know that the Japanese Ambassador had taught our feathered friend some choice English swear words (we were amazed he knew them himself: I didn't know some of them, I have to say, so it was quite an education). This meant that Michael had to make sure that this undiplomatic representative of the avian community was safely out of earshot when there were guests, in case they were offended. But it's staggering how parrot's voices carry. In the end a cover over the cage was the only way to shut it up!

The second thing I remember vividly was standing at the bottom of the Residence garden, in the pouring rain, at 1am on 10th September, trying to light a brazier so I could burn a whole load of secret files. I didn't have much success, as you will read 'Civil Wars'.

Putting a brave face on things. Our very sad farewell to our locally employed (Michael far right).

And lastly, we held the saddest farewell reception of all in the Residence just before we had to leave Guatemala. All the furniture was covered in dust sheets and most of us, including our locally employed, were in floods of tears much of the time. How we all hated to leave them, but we had no choice but to go.

CHILE

The Residence, Las Condes, Santiago

In contrast to the Embasssy, the Residence in Santiago was yet another dignified and stylish building with a large garden at the rear.

Previously owned by the well-heeled property developers, the Sanchez family, 96 Gertrudis Echeñique, Las Condes, had come on the market in 1965 It was suffering from earthquake damage, but we purchased it in 1966 for £90,000, and set about repairing and upgrading it, which we finished in 1967.

There was also an adjacent site which we had purchased in 1972 with a view to building the Embassy there, but this never materialised and we sold it in 1989 for around £2 million. A good profit. I'm sure the Treasury were delighted.

The one down side of the Residence was that an apartment tower block had been built on land adjacent to it, which the Sanchez family also owned. This block was really too close for comfort as people on the top floors could see into the grounds quite easily, so there was little privacy. But it didn't stop us from enjoying the large swimming pool which the Ambassador let us use at stipulated times, provided he wasn't entertaining. I did so often, and it was very welcome.

I also stayed at The Residence for three days when I came out of hospital after a minor operation, as Jennifer was not happy for me to go back to my flat alone. I was extremely grateful to her, and the Ambassador, and I recuperated much quicker as a result.

The rear of the Residence, showing the adjacent apartment block

I was fortunate to attend numerous dinner parties and receptions here at the Residence. The Embassy received a great many visitors, VIPs, and captains of industry, and the Ambassador and Jennifer were excellent hosts. This turned out to be my happiest posting.

MEXICO

In contrast to our elegant Embassy in downtown DF (Distrito Federal as Mexico City is called), I thought the Residence at 1548 Avenida

The Residence, 1548 Avenida Virreyes, Lomas, Mexico City

Virreyes, Lomas, was not very attractive. But Lomas is an affluent residential area in the hills surrounding the DF, regarded as being a safer location during earthquakes than downtown Manila because the houses here are built on bedrock as opposed to the soft jelly like surface of the former *Lago Tenóchtitlán* that the DF rests on. Lomas is also above the level of pollution, always a major problem in the DF. Most of our own homes were/are in this area, and my own super bungalow was not too far away. The majority of other countries' Residences are here also.

Built on land that formed part of the Rancho de Coscoacoaco (you get used to these Aztec names!), the original site was steeply wooded, with old buildings at the bottom, and caves apparently. We bought it in 1959 from a Señora Ofelia Padrón de Piñeda for £46,000.

There then followed deliberations as to what to build there, but it was eventually agreed that it had to be a three-storey house because of the sloping terrain (main reception rooms on the entrance level, with

66

private quarters below on the ground level, and bedrooms at the top). The Treasury also agreed to a swimming pool – eventually – and the Residence was finally finished in 1965 at a cost of £200,000. The Ambassador moved in the next year.

The rear of the Residence, Mexico City
Above: When I was there from 1987-1991
Below: Today (thanks to Mark for the photos)

As I said, to me the house was not very appealing. There are no windows at the front. However, the rear is slightly better, much more so now with all the foliage to soften its appearance. There are manicured lawns, and an oval swimming pool with changing rooms which we could use when convenient. On one occasion when I was there, the Ambassador (John Morgan) dived in, hit his head on the bottom and damaged his neck and spine, necessitating the use of a neck brace for a while. I know it gave him a lot of pain, and I don't think he ever quite recovered.

Inside, the Residence was pleasant, but I felt it lacked atmosphere and charm. However, once again we had some fantastic receptions, dinners, and parties here, my favourite guest being Sir David Attenborough, who came to see the Monarch butterflies. As he was from Leicester too, we had quite a chat. Such a delightful man! The Duke of Edinburgh was also a visitor; and John Morgan held a party for the 'Licence to Kill' cast and crew of course (read on). My new Ambassador, Michael Simpson Orlebar, and his wife Rosita, also gave me a wonderful farewell lunch (as you will have seen in 'My Bosses'). So, I do have fond memories of this Residence, though I usually hurried through the front door and tended not to notice the interior décor too much!

HUNGARY

The Residence, Lorántffy Zsuzsanna utca, Városmajor, Budapest

This beautiful Residence is without doubt my favourite. Situated in the hills of Buda, across the Danube from Pest, where the Embassy was, this is where most of us lived. The villa is elegance personified, both inside and out. The street on which it is located is named after Zsuzsanna (Susanna) Lorántffy (1602-1660), the Princess Consort to György Rákóczi 1, the Prince of Transylvania. She was a passionate Calvinist who helped her husband in his successful struggle to introduce Protestant reforms in the Transylvanian church.

Built in 1925, this stunning neo-baroque villa was the home of Hanna Hódosi and her husband Tibor Scitovszky. Tibor was Undersecretary in the Hungarian Ministry of Commerce and was also economic adviser to the Hungarian delegation at the Trianon peace negotiations after the First World War. He was Minister of Foreign Affairs from 1924-25, then President of the Hungarian General Bank of Credit, and he entered the Upper House of the Hungarian Parliament in 1927.

Hanna and Tibor remained in the house until 1946, when they went to live in the United States. They leased the house to the British Government for use as the Ambassador's Residence, but it was expropriated by the Hungarian Government when the Scitovszky's decided to remain in the States. However, HMG continued to lease it, finally purchasing it in 1964. The interior is just as fine as the exterior, with a magnificent, spiraled staircase and very ornate wrought iron banister. We still own the house today, for which I am eternally grateful. Whatever the function, this villa never fails to impress,

I, and I'm sure my colleagues also, had some wonderful times here. Dinners, parties, receptions for Royal visitors – the functions were legendary. The Ambassador very kindly hosted a lunch for Mum and Dad when they visited me, as well as my own farewell reception. And the QBP invitations were highly prized, with the Ambassador (John Birch) and his wife, Prim, being the most superb host and hostess.

I also remember that when I arrived there was a very ornate koi carp fishpond, complete with lilies, which the Ambassador, somehow, persuaded OED (and, surprisingly, the Treasury) to agree to pay for it to be enlarged and turned into a swimming pool.

There was much correspondence on the subject, which kept me busy for weeks! The only stipulation was that Hungarian labour had to be used to dig it out, which proved to be a mammoth task. But it was an essential staff amenity, we argued, and staff morale would be maintained and enhanced as a result – which it most definitely was. We were ecstatic, and certainly made sure we used it as much as we were allowed to (just to prove it was value for money which, again, it was).

Side view of the Residence down to the swimming pool, Budapest

And, of course, there was *Istvan*, the Ambassador's amazing butler. A tall, imposing man, he was calm, dignified, and super-efficient. Softly spoken, with excellent English, he was indispensable, and he and I worked very closely together during my time in Budapest. I could always rely on him, as of course could the Ambassador, and things went like clockwork. I often wonder what became of him. He was younger than me (nearly everyone seems younger these days), so whether he is still alive or not, I don't know. I must enquire.

Whenever I have entered one of our Residences abroad, I have been extremely proud to do so. Some may not be to my 'traditional' taste, but each one reflects HMG's continuing importance in the world.

1993 QBP. UK based staff and wives.
(I'm second row, fifth from left)

Our thanks must go to OED for looking after them so well. I know their maintenance takes up a lot of time and resources and can be a real headache. And, yes, our thanks must even go to the Treasury for continuing to pay for their purchase and upkeep!

Exceedingly good investments. Money well spent, I say.

Chapter Seven

My Own Accommodation

Moving somewhat down market from Residences, having arrived at Post, I needed to sort out my own accommodation. In Peru, Mexico and Hungary, it was arranged for me. I occupied the flat or house my predecessor or another colleague had lived in. In the Philippines, Guatemala and Chile I had to find my own.

THE PHILIPPINES

My new home - 59a Paseo de Roxas, Makati Manila

I did not have a very good beginning. As the Embassy had moved from downtown Manila up to the new commercial area of Makati, the lease on my predecessor's flat was terminated and somewhere else needed to be found for me to live. I initially went into the Mandarin Hotel, near the Embassy, but it seemed a house owned by the aunt of one of the Admin Section locally employed staff had been identified as suitable and agreed by the H of C. I went to look at it and was absolutely appalled. I flatly refused to occupy it. It was in a somewhat run-down residential area of Manila called Buendia and was away from the rest of my UK based colleagues. The house had a small concrete backyard with jagged glass on top of the high walls surrounding it; barred windows; a pipe sticking out of the wall in the kitchen (no sign of a tap); small rooms; and big iron gates at the front. Security was obviously a problem in this area, and I knew I wouldn't feel safe here. I asked my boss, Peter, to come and have a look. When he saw it, he agreed that there was no way I was going to live there. Poor Bill was at a loss to understand why I didn't like it, but I was adamant. I hadn't come 10,728 miles to spend the next three years of my life out on a limb, in an unsafe area, living in a house which fell far short of anything else in which my colleagues lived. And that was that!

So I remained in the hotel and spent all my lunch hours and after work with an estate agent going around Makati trying to find a flat or house that was suitable.

Eventually I decided on part of a bungalow, 59a Paseo de Roxas, near to the Mandarin Hotel, on the edge of Urdaneta Village, a very pleasant gated residential urbanization not too far from the Embassy. The rent was within the allowance for my grade and, more to the point, Bill agreed it was adequate. As an added bonus, the New Zealand Ambassador's PA. Lorna, lived in the middle part of the bungalow. We became very good friends, and still are. I rarely saw the occupants on the other side of Lorna.

It wasn't ideal. It had no garden, and the front door was the patio doors on the left, not so good for security as I was to find out when I went on leave. It had two bedrooms, one small kitchen, a bathroom with black tiles, and a lounge-cum-dining room. The furnishings were not quite to my taste, but with my own additions I could live with that. It was all we could find for the price, was infinitely better than the house in Buendia, and so I moved in.

I was burgled during my mid-tour leave, and lost nearly everything, especially all my electrical goods. Both padlocks on the patio doors had been cut through, and I'm sure it was the janitor who was responsible. Only he (and Lorna) knew I was away, and he knew how to get in. I couldn't prove it, of course, but he looked very shifty when I got back and did his best to steer clear of me from then onwards. Despite all this, though, I did enjoy living there and have fond memories.

PERU

6th floor, Avenida Benavides, Lima (the middle block)

Lima was much better. I took over my predecessor's flat on the sixth floor of a block on Avenida Benavides in the very smart residential area of Miraflores, where the Embassy is today. There were two flats to each floor and I had lovely neighbours, - the *familia Biber Sherpa* - with their teenage son. My flat was spacious, with a lounge, dining room, two bedrooms, kitchen, an inside bathroom, and an outside utility area at the back. The Embassy furniture was tasteful, and it felt very homely. But most of all, it had superb views, and I could even see (between other blocks of flats) and walk to the sea. It had a rear car park, was ideally situated near the shops, and was not too far from the ring road I had to take to get to work.

I really liked this flat and was so sorry to leave it.

GUATEMALA

12th floor of the block on the right, Avenida La Reforma, Guatemala City

The lease had expired on my predecessor's flat in Guatemala City, which meant I had to find my own place to live. I trudged around, again with an estate agent, in my time off and eventually identified a twelfth floor flat in the residential area Zona 10, on Avenida La Reforma. Again, the views were superb – the best I ever had – but the flat was not large. I wasn't too keen on the furniture either, but had I stayed there longer, I could have bought items more to my taste.

I didn't know any of my neighbours. We British weren't very popular because of the situation over Belize, and at the end, knowing we were being expelled when Belize gained its Independence, they were positively rude.

I don't know how I would have got on had I stayed longer. I don't have particularly fond memories of that flat.

CHILE

More flat hunting. By now I was getting quite good at this, and Spanish estate agent jargon just tripped off my tongue. As you will read in the Conflicts chapter, again I had a rather fraught beginning and had only just moved in when the Falklands Conflict started.

6th floor, Avenida Suecia, Providencia, Santiago

But at least I had had time to find a really lovely flat, again on the sixth floor, of a fairly modern, well-constructed block on Avenida Suecia, in the affluent suburb of Providencia, not too far from the Embassy. I was so happy here. There were four flats on each floor, and I had the one on the right at the rear. Again, the views were amazing - the ski slopes at *El Colorado* from the side, and a wonderful panorama of Providencia and downtown Santiago to the rear. It was spacious, with two bedrooms, a lounge-cum-dining room, kitchen, bathroom and outside utility area, but more importantly for me, it had a lovely balcony with rattan blinds where I could just chill out. The block was built to withstand earthquakes, but did sway quite a bit during them, which was somewhat disconcerting. Thankfully we remained in one piece. If there was one slight downside, it was the b....... cockerel next door which was an early riser to say the least. I viewed him longingly at Christmas. How lucky he was!

Again, I was so sad to leave my Chilean home. Pam came to stay twice, and I also had other visitors. I even hosted some really good dinner parties, so I'm told. And my newly acquired budgie liked it!

MEXICO

My bungalow, 128a Sierra Amatepec, Lomas de Chapultepec, Mexico City

Without doubt, my bungalow in Lomas de Chapultepec, in the foothills outside Mexico City, was by far my best accommodation. I had taken it over from my predecessor, and I absolutely loved it.

My parking area was at the front of a two-storey house divided into four flats, and to reach my own bungalow I had to go through a hallway and then down to the bottom of their garden, where there were steps leading to my own garden, the end of which was perched on the edge of a deep *barranca* (ravine - not good for snakes, I found out to my consternation). When I arrived, this outside area was very overgrown, but I could see it had potential. As I like gardening, I asked my excellent landlady if I do some work on it. She was absolutely delighted and gave me free rein to do whatever I liked. So I, and my wonderful *portero,* Cándido (the caretaker – whose wages were paid for by my landlady) set to work transforming my garden into a colourful, tranquil sanctuary where I

Cándido

could relax, sunbathe in privacy, and hold lunches and dinner parties on the decorative patio outside my French windows. Cándido was thrilled to have some gardening to do. He and I would go off at weekends to the vast market garden at *Xochimilco* and come back with a car full of bougainvilleas, azalias, hibiscus – anything vibrant that would grow at this altitude and in this soil. It wasn't Kew, but the result was beautiful, and my landlady was amazed.

I spent a great deal of time outside when the weather permitted (it did get quite cold in winter), and I particularly loved to sit on the patio, beneath the shade of the willow tree from which I hung my hummingbird feeders. These amazing little birds became quite used to me and were my constant companions, their wings whirring away as they sucked at the special nectar I had bought to fill the feeders.

Inside, the bungalow was spacious, with a white (once) shag pile carpet throughout. The only downside to this was that it trapped the scorpions coming in from their nest under the patio step, which necessitated buying a pair of industrial gloves to remove them. In the end Cándido blocked up the hole and that solved that problem (sorry scorpions). I then only had to deal with the geckos,

My lounge in the evening sunlight

which became unstuck from the bedroom walls and plopped with great frequency onto me in the middle of the night, scaring me to death!

There were two bedrooms, a large kitchen and outside drying area, a bathroom and lovely lounge. Pam came again to stay twice and loved the house too.

I had some wonderful times at *Sierra Amatepec*. Just looking at these photographs revives so many happy memories.

Both Cándido and I cried when it was time for me to say *adíos*. I never gave him extra money as he tended to use it to go on 'benders' now and then, but I had given him things for his family and daughters in particular who lived away in the country, and had helped him read and write when necessary. He had been indispensable to me during my three years in Mexico, the only time I had had someone to count on or help me at home. I knew I would miss him a lot. And I did.

Adíos to my very happy home

HUNGARY

Napvirag utca, Budapest, and Erno Rubik (thanks for the photo, Erno)

Prior to my arrival in Budapest, all of our staff had been housed in in compounds (full of bugs, of both kinds!). At the end of Communism, we were allowed to rent private properties around Budapest and a flat had been identified as a possible home for me on *The Var*. This was an ideal tourist location, but not so ideal for living there with the numerous coaches stopping outside the flat to disgorge ever increasing numbers of sightseers. It was noisy (I'm a light sleeper), and the pollution was becoming a bit of a problem too. However, Tony, our single Security Officer, was very happy to live there, so it was agreed that I would have the flat he was to live in, and he would have mine.

I went to live in a Rubik cube! My landlord was none other than Erno Rubik, and my flat was very square. He was lovely: quiet and unassuming, a Math's Professor, and he was very keen to make sure I was comfortable, and everything ran smoothly. I got to know him reasonably well during my time in Budapest.

There were five flats in the block Erno owned (I don't know how long he had owned it, but it couldn't have been long). Four were at street level, and one was a large basement garden flat occupied by the Szabo family.

I lived in the right hand ground floor flat, the top two being boarded up for some reason, which suited me fine as I had no-one stamping around above me. It wasn't over large but was adequate. It had a galley kitchen, two bedrooms, a bathroom with brown tiles and a lounge leading onto a balcony with a superb view over the Buda hills.

My balcony at Napvirag utca, and views over the Buda hills

When I first arrived my neighbours, especially Mr and Mrs Horvath in the flat adjoining mine, treated me with suspicion and resentment. They were not used to foreigners, and here was a single lady occupying a flat that normally a family would live in. To make matters worse, I had a new car (my Escort) and they had a clapped out Lada and a Trabant. This didn't go down well at all, even though I had taken out a loan to buy it. My Hungarian was none too good either, though their English was better. But I persevered, taking my turn on the rubbish bin roster, and anything else that needed doing.

I asked if I could plant roses in the two beds at the front, which left them completely baffled. No-one had any pride in anything, so it seemed. However, it did make a difference, and they agreed it looked nice when I had finished. I helped the Szabo's teenage daughters with their English, and ran errands for Mr and Mrs Horvath, who were elderly. Slowly I became accepted. .

I had to appreciate that it was a tough time for the Hungarians now that Communism had ended. Life had become very uncertain for them, especially the middle-aged and elderly. They had been brought up 'in the system' with a guaranteed job in unprofitable businesses. Now everything had changed, and they were fearful.

In the end we became good friends. I said goodbye to Erno and thanked him profusely for his diligence in looking after me and the flat. He was very pleased. My neighbors gave me a very unexpected but welcome farewell party, and I kept in touch with the Szabos for a little while after I left Budapest.

It had been an interesting experience, and I had learned a lot from my time with them all, for which I am grateful

The Hungarian Customs Officer signing my release papers after he had inspected my baggage at home.

PART FIVE

The Ambassador's PA

INVESTOR IN PEOPLE

Foreign &
Commonwealth Office

Human Resources Directorate
Old Admiralty Building
London SW1A 2PA

Telephone: (020) 7008 0579/80
Facsimile: (020) 7008 0581
E-mail: David.Warren@fco.gov.uk

7 April 2005

Ms Gillian Angrave
WLD
W111D

Dear Gillian,

Your imminent retirement brings to an end your career of 29 years in the Diplomatic Service. I am writing on behalf of the Office to thank you for all your work during your time with us. You have made a great contribution to the work of the Office, and we shall be sorry to say goodbye.

After you joined the Service in 1976 you served in a variety of posts in the secretarial cadre at home and overseas, including Manila, Lima, Guatemala City, Santiago, Mexico City, and Budapest. For the last 10 years you have held senior PA posts in London.

You approached each job with impeccable professionalism, and justifiably took pride in setting the highest possible standards. Reliable, efficient, interested, and fastidious on detail, you took everything in your stride with enthusiasm and good humour. An engaging approachability and excellent skills as a thoughtful and supportive team player made you an enormously popular and valued colleague. You earned many accolades from your Reporting Officers – "a Rolls Royce service"; "outstandingly effective, polished and professional in the best traditions of the Service"; "a very friendly, calm and reliable presence at the centre of the Command " are typical examples. You will be greatly missed by colleagues and friends across the Service and I hope that you will keep in touch with them.

The Service relies enormously on the dedication, professionalism and flair of its members – qualities you have so amply demonstrated. As you look back over your career, I hope it is with a sense of achievement and pride in a job well done. You will be much missed. I wish you all the very best for a long and happy retirement.

With all good wishes,

Yours ever,

David Warren
Director, Human Resources

My valedictory letter from the FCO upon my retirement in 2005

Chapter Eight

My Erstwhile 'Bosses' – (From My Side of the Desk)

It may seem a little odd to start this Chapter with my valedictory letter from the FCO in 2005, but it has a bearing on what follows. Throughout my time in the Diplomatic Service, I always tried to give of my best, both to my bosses and to that Service which I loved so much. There were a few hiccups along the way, as you will see, but I'm proud of the job I did, of the service I gave, and of what David Warren wrote. To know that one is appreciated makes it all seem so worthwhile.

First and foremost, I have had the great privilege and pleasure (mostly) of working for some brilliant, inspiring Ambassadors. Their command of the English language - both written and verbal - has been truly staggering. They would outshine 'Sir Humphrey' any day! I think this is why I have been minded to write my books. They have had such an influence on my life, and I would like to think that some of their expertise (even a tiny amount) has rubbed off on me. I learned a lot from them, for which I will always be grateful.

As I referred to in my Preface, [Sir] John Birch, my favourite Ambassador (in Budapest), when reviewing my *Memoir* wrote that I had a 'kind and lucid pen'. I have tried to remain true to his words whilst writing this book, and hope I have done so. I don't believe in settling old scores. But there are one or two instances when, with justification, I might be slightly less generous than normal. For example, when, pounding away on my old Remington typewriter, re-doing the Annual Review for the seventh time because of one small mistake (theirs, not mine!), having to correct all eight carbon copies with a rubber (no Tipp-Ex allowed), then my feelings of *bonhomie* and goodwill may have been somewhat lacking. But those feelings usually only lasted for a few moments, unless I was having a particularly bad day.

Whilst some of those for whom I worked back in London are still alive, and I'm so pleased to be touch with a few, I'm also conscious that all my 'foreign' Ambassadors are no longer with us, and therefore are not able to answer for themselves. Some wouldn't have deigned to do so anyway, and they may have viewed things slightly differently. But this is **my** story, from **my** side of the desk, so when things get a little fraught, I'm going to say so. I've decided to take each country in turn. So here goes.

The Philippines

When I arrived in Manila in 1976, James Turpin was the Ambassador, though he was only there for two months or so before he retired, so I didn't really know him at all. He was replaced by [Sir] William (Bill) Bentley.

As this was my first posting, and the timing suited The Office, I was sent to work for Peter George, Counsellor/Consul-General, and Chargé in the Ambassador's absence. I really liked Peter, and his French wife, Andrée. They were very kind, supportive and considerate. We were always extremely busy, and life was hectic, especially on the commercial front, which Peter oversaw, but they always had time for me. I got the impression that Peter was glad that I was an 'older' PA who had travelled extensively beforehand, and had some experience of the commercial world, having worked for The Rank Organisation, an architect, an engineering and iron foundry company, American Marine yacht company, Winthrop Stearns and, of course, P&O, before joining The Office. This gave me a broader outlook on life than perhaps one of the younger, new PAs, might have had. I was regularly asked to attend Peter's dinner parties and receptions, which I always did with the greatest pleasure. It was very useful, both to Peter and to me, to know to whom I was talking on the phone, or meeting as part of my work. I found this particularly so with my knowledge of Spanish when posted to South American countries.

I learned to play golf in the Philippines, and had an exceptionally good pro, Carlos, with whom I became great friends. Peter enjoyed golf too, so I was very pleased to introduce him to Carlos who helped him a lot with his game.

Peter retired, and I left Manila, at about the same time in 1980. He and Andreé both died some years ago.

Bill Bentley, the Ambassador, and his Danish wife, Karen, were also very pleasant. He was a good host, and again I much enjoyed being invited to his dinner parties along with his PA, Ann Douthwaite, with whom I'm still in touch. Ann and I became good friends, and we travelled around the Philippines quite a bit together when time allowed.

The Ambassador (we never called them by their Christian name) was a very keen and excellent fisherman who even had a fishing fly named after him. He also enjoyed shooting, though he wasn't quite so good at that. This was particularly evident at our Christmas parties at the Residence. Instead of turkey, stuffing, roast potatoes and all the trimmings, which I personally longed for, we were served a dish of sticky coated snipe, complete with lead shot. This necessitated a hasty visit straight to the bar to take a generous swig of wine, imported from Hong Kong at great expense. Who cares? I most certainly didn't!

On one occasion, when I was Duty Officer, I had to go into the Embassy at 0400 on a Sunday morning to get him five boxes of cartridges for his day's sport (snipe)! Not to worry. That's what we PA's are there for! By the time I had shut up the Embassy, I was late for my round of golf and played like a drain anyway.

Bill Bentley retired in 1987. Sadly, he drowned during a flash flood whilst fishing in the River Usk. Although he was doing something he loved, I can only imagine his terror as he was swept away. Such a tragic end to a distinguished life.

Peru

My thanks go to our excellent H of C in Lima, Denis Doble (he and his wife Patricia have remained my friends ever since then), for putting me right on a few points here and there of which I was unaware at the time.

I arrived in Peru in May 1980, absolutely thrilled to be posted there, and much looking forward to a very happy two and a half year stay in that fascinating country.

I was warmly greeted by the Ambassador, Charles Wallace, a small man, half Spanish, half Scottish, with an interesting mix of temperaments. He was, of course, bilingual, and ideally suited to be Ambassador in a South American country. His wife, Gloria, was Guatemalan, and I liked her a lot, though I think she sometimes had a rather difficult time with her husband.

The Ambassador and I seemed to be getting on well. I worked hard, and he was pleased that I had a good knowledge of Spanish which enabled him to dictate letters to me in that language, although I knew no Spanish shorthand and had to write them in longhand. Socially he was excellent, and I attended some really enjoyable receptions at the Residence, though not as many dinner parties as in the Philippines.

However, the main drawback was his disposition: he had a very short fuse and was quick to get into quite a rage. He was more Spanish than Scottish in that respect. Often, my colleagues would find themselves in the doghouse, and at times it was difficult to fit any more in. I managed to stay out of the kennel for a long time, but then things began to go wrong, and I went in there too.

I continued to work hard, though, and the Ambassador genuinely seemed pleased with what I did. One thing I didn't have to worry about was the social side of my job. The Ambassador had a Social Secretary, Gladys, who took care of sending out invitations and organizing dinner parties, which freed me up to concentrate on everything else.

Not all Missions have a Social Secretary: the large ones do, and they are allowed for in the Ambassador's *frais* - his allowance for the entertaining side of his job. But otherwise, it is at the Ambassador's discretion whether to have one or not. Social Secretaries are locally employed, but occasionally a wife will take on that role, which is ideal because they are more familiar with the content.

I got on well with my colleagues; and socially I was an asset with my Spanish, but I soon became the Ambassador's 'whipping boy' for anything that didn't go according to plan, whether it was my fault or not, and it began to take its toll on my health. I started to dread going into the Embassy, wondering what the day had in store for me. On one occasion, I was on the receiving end of a stapler hurled at me in rage (not through anything I had done, but after a telephone call which he didn't like). It hit me on the head, whereupon I got up, walked out of my office, and refused to go back until he apologized, which he did, profusely. Man-management was not one of his *fortes,* I had come to realize.

The situation quickly deteriorated. I've been trying to analyse, over the years, when and why this started to happen. Denis said it quickly became a clash of personalities. I was a perfectly competent PA (and never had any problems anywhere else), but the Ambassador's demanding, and often unfair, attitude became increasingly hard to cope with. I think perhaps it was also because, at thirty-five, I was an older entrant (as Miss Lofting had said on my first day); had had a varied career in industry and at sea before joining the FCO, and I wasn't used to this sort of treatment. I let it be known as diplomatically as I could that I was not happy about it, but it seemed to make no difference. I do feel - and I'm not alone in this - that a few Ambassadors, once away from London, became little tin Gods in their own little 'kingdoms'. This usually meant it was not a happy Embassy to work in.

Denis was a tower of strength during this challenging period. He was very supportive, even though he found the Ambassador quite difficult at times. He also became mediator *par excellence* between the Ambassador and our First Secretary Commercial (Peter Pendleton). Peter and Charles Wallace had been together in their previous posting in Asunción (Paraguay), where things had definitely turned very sour. I gather the Ambassador's CMG was held up as a result. He created such a fuss that he was eventually awarded the 'gong'. Peter was subsequently posted to Lima, but to his horror Charles Wallace turned up again as Ambassador there, and so the feud continued.

Our Embassy doctor, Dr Zapff, was such a comfort too – my *confidant* – particularly when he admitted me to hospital for two days with nervous exhaustion. In the meantime, Denis had contacted POD insisting, as best he could, that I be moved. I was heartbroken. I loved Peru; had managed to get out and about travelling when I could; and desperately wanted to stay. But whatever I did, things didn't seem to be getting any better and, worst of all, I still couldn't work out what I was doing wrong.

I understand from Denis that POD were very sympathetic to his recommendation, but it was taking a little while for them to identify another suitable posting for me (of which I was unaware at the time). By now I knew that I wouldn't be able to put up this sort of treatment for the rest of my tour (why should I?), and that I would have to leave. I remember on one occasion crying on the shoulder of Cecil Parkinson, the visiting Trade Secretary, when he was in my office asking if I was enjoying my posting. I said no. He wanted to know why, and then the tears flowed as I blurted out what was happening. I said I'd had enough and felt I had no option but to leave. He was very concerned, spoke to the H of C, I gather, but there was nothing he could do.

It even got to the stage when one night I went into the Embassy and sent a telex to POD saying that if they didn't take me out of Peru, I'd jump out of the 12th floor window. Not that I would ever have done so: that is not me (and anyway the windows didn't open). But drastic times needed drastic measures, and that was all I could think of.

POD at last identified another posting for me, and the Ambassador reluctantly (?) agreed that I could be cross-posted within a few weeks to Guatemala, working as PA to Michael Wilmshurst, the Consul-General and Head of Post there, the Mission having been downgraded from an Embassy because of the problems over Belize. The vacancy had just occurred because Michael's PA was leaving unexpectedly for personal reasons, and as Guatemala was 'in the area' so to speak, this seemed an ideal solution. I was very relieved, and really pleased that I would remain in a Spanish-speaking environment. But I was still devastated to be leaving my colleagues and a country I had come to love.

I started to pack and spent the last two weeks working for Denis as it was decided, for continuity purposes, that his PA and I would swap jobs. The Ambassador and I parted on amicable terms, and I finally boarded the Eastern Airlines flight to Miami, where I was spending three days with my good friend, Pat, who lived there, before travelling on to Guatemala.

Subsequently, I met the Ambassador again when I travelled up to Lima from Santiago, where I was later posted, for a few days' holiday. He couldn't have been nicer. He sat me down, gave me a cup of tea, and wanted to know how I was and what I had been doing. He seemed genuinely interested, and I reciprocated with equal warmth. It took a bit of doing, but I'm not one to bear grudges as I said, and I began to feel that he truly didn't realize how badly he had treated me. Still, I'm pleased we said goodbye on such good terms.

Charles Wallace eventually left Peru in 1983 under something of a cloud over his handling of the Peruvian Peace Plan during the Falklands Conflict. It seemed that he only learned of this initiative on his car radio (that wretched car radio: how we all came to loathe it) and relayed it to London three hours after the sinking of the Argentinian light cruiser *General Belgrano*. However, President Belaunde, with whom he and his wife were extremely friendly, believes otherwise. He was subsequently posted to Montevideo until 1985, which to me seems a bit of a demotion, though he was well placed to try to influence Argentinian attitudes. (This is all well documented, so I won't comment on it further.)

Charles Wallace died in 2014.

I also understand now from Denis that he and I just missed working together again in Santiago, which I would have much welcomed. Charles Wallace had given him a very good report, mainly for all his help during the Falklands Conflict, and POD had recommended that Denis be posted to Chile as Counsellor after John Hughes. However, Denis was anxious to get back to South Asia, which he loved, and so he hesitated. He went back to London on a home posting for two years and was eventually posted to Bombay as Acting Deputy High Commissioner. Thank you for all you did for me in Peru, though, Denis. It made such a difference.

Guatemala

Feeling slightly 'battered' when I arrived in Guatemala, I was apprehensive as to what I would encounter there as the country was in the grip of a bloody Civil War. I imagine Michael (Wilmshurst) would have been aware of the circumstances of my departure from Lima, and perhaps he, too, wondered what he was letting himself in for by agreeing to my posting as his PA! But, for me, what a contrast he was to Charles Wallace! He restored my faith in human nature by a long margin. He was so very kind, considerate, supportive, and remained calm amidst all the turmoil we were facing. We worked extremely well together, and I liked him a lot, as did my colleagues. His wife, Mary, was a so easy to get on with too. She was an excellent hostess and was such a help to me when I got so sick.

We were only a very small Mission, but I established a good rapport with my colleagues, and we worked well as a team, fielding off one crisis after another.

As my friends will tell you, I'm a great fan of Victor Meldrew (played brilliantly by Richard Wilson) in 'One Foot in the 'Grave', and I've had cause to use his famous utterance on numerous occasions. This was another one! Things were going swimmingly, when we were expelled from Guatemala over Belizean Independence, and we had only three days to leave the country. *I DON'T BELIEVE IT!*. Not another short tour. This wasn't quite what I had in mind when I joined the Diplomatic Service. However, I believe resilience and flexibility in times of hardship are qualities that are looked for in members of the Diplomatic Service at our interviews. I certainly needed those qualities then, and many times in the future!

Michael Joseph Wilmshurst died on 12 October 2006.

Chile

John Moore Heath CMG

John Hickman CMG presenting his
Letters of Credence (Credentials)
To General Augusto Pinochet

After my unexpected arrival in London in September 1981, POD then had to look for another posting for me. I was elated when they told me that my next posting would be Santiago in February 1982, and that I would be PA to the Ambassador, John Moore Heath.

He again was exceptionally pleasant, and we got on well, as I did with his wife Patricia. But he was retiring in April, so we wouldn't have much time together, sadly.

Enter Victor Meldrew once more! I'd been in Santiago six weeks when the Falklands Conflict started. Oh no! *I DON'T BELIEVE IT!* What have I done to deserve all this? It meant, of course, that the Ambassador had to postpone his retirement until after the Conflict had ended, which I personally was very glad about, even if he wasn't.

I then got ready for my new Ambassador, John Hickman (and his wife, Jennifer, whom I liked), who was coming to Chile having been Ambassador to Ecuador beforehand. We got on well, though he did have his idiosyncrasies (don't we all?), one of which was that he took snuff, particularly when I was taking dictation. I quite liked the aroma of the spices, but he had a habit of blowing the powder off his hand so that it went all over me, causing me to have sneezing fits, and turning my blouses pink! Never mind. Remember Gillian - resilience and flexibility!

He was also writing a book on the Galapagos Islands ('The Enchanted Islands: The Galapagos Discovered') on which he was an expert. This was great. I found the subject fascinating and was happy to type the odd chapter for him after work. But it got to the stage when it looked as if I was set to type the whole book for him in my time off, for no extra pay, which I didn't think was really fair. I had better things to do after work, like a round of golf at the Prince of Wales Country Club, or a trip to the Irish pub nearby! So eventually I suggested that Elspeth, his Social Secretary, might like to type the chapters for him, having checked with her first. He readily agreed and I heaved a sigh of relief. But he didn't realize, and I didn't enlighten him, that Elspeth, who was locally employed, expected to be paid the going rate for this extra work. This didn't go down too well at all, but such is life. He eventually got over the shock and she finished the book for him. He did give me a signed copy when it was published, thanking me for what I had done. I was delighted and I still have that book to this day.

One further thought on this. Now I'm writing myself, how glad I am that I can type. Think of all the money I save!

The Ambassador somewhat blotted his copybook towards the end of his tour. I won't go into detail as it is documented, but it involved importing high spec cars at diplomatic rates and selling them off at a great profit. Whilst this wasn't illegal, it was unethical, and eventually he was asked to stop, both by the Chileans and by London.

Personally, I found what he was doing very galling. As I was due a home posting after Santiago, I was saving hard for a deposit on a flat.

Because I had taken out an FCO car loan to buy my Escort, the rules were that if I made a profit, I had to repay The Office half. I made £200 profit from the sale of my car, and I had to return £100 to London. I shall say no more!

However, I did enjoy working for the Ambassador and Chile was my happiest posting. Reluctantly I left there in1985 and returned to the UK, but the memories of my time there will never leave me.

John Kyle Hickman died in 2001, aged 73.

Mexico

When I arrived in in Mexico in 1987 after my home posting, my Ambassador was John Morgan (wife, Angela). He welcomed me warmly, as did my UK colleagues and the locally employed, and I instantly felt part of the team. I had a small office adjoining the Ambassador's at the front of the Embassy, and we worked well together, though I did find him a bit 'cold' at times. But this didn't matter. Resilience and flexibility to the fore, again, Gillian. I was by now becoming very used to my Ambassadors' different idiosyncrasies!

There were two occasions, though, when I was a bit 'put out'! One was when I had to have a hysterectomy at the American British Cowdray Hospital in Mexico City, and I needed to take five weeks sick leave as a result (a floater covered for me during this time). The Ambassador was chafing at the bit to get me back to work, and I did so as soon as I had my surgeon's clearance to do so. But on my first day back he wanted a large number of files carried backwards and forwards between his office and the Registry and was none too pleased when I explained that I would have to do so in stages as I still couldn't carry anything really heavy. "But you're back at work" he said. "Yes," I said. "I'll do my best, but for the moment I have to be a bit careful." I was doing my best and felt somewhat aggrieved. I also considered ringing Angela up and asking her to explain the situation in detail to her husband!

The other occasion occurred when the Inspectors came out to the Embassy (as they did to all the Embassies in turn over the years) to carry out their comprehensive review of all we were doing and spending, interviewing us all in turn. Meg Rothwell was the Chief Inspector on this occasion, I remember. She sat me down and we had a good chat about how things were going, how I was finding Mexico and the Embassy in particular, and whether I had anything I would like to raise with her. I had. The Ambassador had a locally employed Social Secretary, one of whose jobs was of course to attend to the entertainment side of his role, writing out all the invitation cards to receptions, dinner parties and other events, dealing with the RSVPs and so forth. But increasingly, all this time-consuming work seemed to be landing on my desk instead, greatly adding to my workload and making it difficult for me to keep up at times. I asked Meg why she couldn't do it. She agreed, and spoke to the Ambassador about it, which did not make him, or Angela, very happy. It transpired that she spent all her time at the Residence buying household items and liaising with the servants, thus relieving Angela of a lot of the tedium of being an Ambassador's wife. Fine. But she did have other duties to perform too which, after Meg Rothwell's intervention, she then started to do. Fortunately, she and I got on well and she understood, she said. She knew it was part of her job, but had just done what she was told. I had noticed, though, that she hadn't felt the need to offer to help me! However, all was soon forgotten, and we continued to work well.

Upon leaving Mexico in 1989, John Morgan retired from the Service and was subsequently knighted. He pursued a very active retirement, being amongst other things a Trustee of the British Museum and a Governor of the LSE. He died in 2012.

I then prepared to welcome my new Ambassador, Michael Simpson-Orlebar, and his Colombian wife, Rosita, who had come from Portugal. Again, we got on well and I enjoyed working for him, even if he was somewhat withdrawn at times. He did have a habit of ignoring me completely each morning when he walked through my office to get to his own, which I thought was a bit rude and made me feel like a table, or a chair! I did mention this, but it was not well received, so I just had to put up with it. I still feel, though, that a 'good morning' doesn't cost anything, and can make a big difference to someone's day. However, I did find some strong medication in the fridge one day which made me think he wasn't too well at all (I have since learned that he wasn't), so I made allowances.

The Ambassador (and Rosita) were very hospitable, and I well remember the very nice farewell lunch he gave for me and my closest friends at the Residence when I left Mexico in 1991.

The Ambassador's farewell lunch for me

Michael Simpson Orlebar left Mexico in 1992 and retired from the Service. He was knighted, and died in 2000

Hungary

Good old Victor Meldrew again! *"I DON'T BELIEVE IT!"* About two months before I was due to leave Mexico, the letter came through with my next posting. I was excited as I knew I was being considered for Madrid. I opened the envelope and stared in horror at the destination - **HUNGARY.** What? Why on earth would I want to go there? I wasn't aware they spoke Spanish in Hungary. But that was where I was due to go and, as it happened, that is where I worked for my very favourite Ambassador.

[Sir] John Birch was super. A Quaker, he was so kind, considerate, amusing, and very appreciative of all that I did, and it was a pleasure to go into the Embassy each day. His wife, Prim, was extremely nice too, and it made for a fantastic working atmosphere.

When Mum died, I found in the loft a box containing all the letters I had written to her and Dad throughout my years of travel. I found it very emotional to read them, but I came across one of my 'Christmas Epistles,' sent to them and my friends, that refers to John Birch|:

"The Ambassador is a real sweetheart and we have established a good working relationship right from the start. His wife, Prim, is a lovely lady too. He is kind, unpretentious, extremely young-looking, and considerate to a fault. I even received a lovely bouquet of flowers on my birthday. Best of all, we can have a laugh. He is very particular about appearance - to an exaggerated degree sometimes - but since I tend to be the same as my mother will tell you, we understand each other perfectly. At last, POD, we are getting somewhere!"

We were frantically busy. It was just at the end of Communism and there was so much to do on the political side: new contacts to cultivate; extensive reporting on the new political scene after the first free parliamentary election held in 1990; Royal and VIP visitors galore

Sir John Birch on the steps of the Residence, with his
two Hungarian Vizslas, Flora and Daisy.

and Ambassadorial visits around the country to organize.

And then, to crown it all (forgive the pun), The State Visit of Her Majesty The Queen and HRH the Duke of Edinburgh in May 1993. I thought I knew what hard work was. Wait until a State Visit. You'd be flabbergasted! I've described it all in my chapter on Official Visits, and so won't go into too much detail here. At the end of the day the Visit was an enormous success, and we all felt a great sense of pride, me especially, when the Ambassador received his Knighthood from Her Majesty during that Visit.

However, we couldn't rest on our laurels. Yet more VIPs arrived, and the Ambassador and I worked on steadily together. As there was no Social Secretary as such, I was also fully occupied with his extensive social commitments as well, but for really big functions one of our locally employed helped me as much as she could, for which I was so grateful.

But there was time for fun too. The Ambassador and Prim were extremely hospitable and joined in with everything. What delighted me the most was that they were superb tennis players, and the Ambassador and I partnered each other in all our Embassy tournaments and, I have to say, won the lot - and on our own merits, not because he was the boss (I had had coaching with Mark Cox, but had not been able to continue when I went to sea). I still have the little medals from our successes, which amused the Ambassador a great deal when I told him just before he died.

I was sad to leave the Ambassador, Budapest and Hungary. After all my initial misgivings, I came to realize that Hungary too was facing challenges far more important than mine as the country emerged from the grip of Communism. We were both on a path of discovery and grown together - for a while at least - and learned from each other. It wasn't South America, and there were many problems, but John Birch made my stay there unforgettable and so enjoyable.

Over the years John (as I now called him), Prim and I met up fairly frequently as they lived near the FCO. After I retired from The Office, we still kept in touch, and John was an enormous help and support when I was writing my *Memoir,* as I said. I went for lunch with him and Prim in September 2019. They were planning a trip to India in February (just before the pandemic struck), and I was looking forward to hearing how it all went. But I was devastated to learn on their return that he was seriously ill, and he died on 6 May 2020. I was so, so sad. I spoke to Prim a week or so ago (early December 2022). It was good to talk to her and know that she is well, but missing her husband of course, as do so many. I asked her permission to use the photograph of John that appeared in his Obituary, and she was delighted that I wanted to do so. I won't forget, Prim. Thank you.

The Ambassador, Mum, Dad, and me outside the Residence
when he invited them to lunch during their visit

My Home Posting Bosses

Every five years or so we had to go on a home posting, ostensibly so we didn't get too used to a particular environment, and to keep us abreast of what was going on in The Office and in the UK.

My first spell in London was forced on me. Having been expelled from Guatemala, POD were actively looking for a new posting for me as soon as I arrived, and so I spent the five months there before being posted to Chile filling in for Heads of Departments' PAs who were going on leave, were sick etc. My bosses changed almost daily, and I can't really remember who they all were now, but I do recollect Dominic Asquith telling me that I must NOT shake the Iranian Ambassador's hand when I went to escort him to Dominic's office. A definite cultural no-no. I nearly forgot but remembered just in time.

My first real home posting came in February 1985, after Chile. I was sent to work as PA to **[Dame] Pauline Neville Jones**, Head of Planning Staff, the Department instrumental in formulating foreign policy. It was intense to say the least, as was Pauline, whom I liked and got on well with. This was a Department of high flyers – Judith Macgregor and Mariot Leslie in particular, and we were situated next door to the office of the PUS, Sir Antony Acland (Permanent Under-Secretary of State and Civil Service Head of the FCO), with unlimited access to him. Pauline was brilliant at her job, and although we worked very long hours, I found the job and the process of policy-making both enlightening and rewarding.

However, after eighteen months in Planning Staff, it was time for a move, and I then went to work for **[Sir] Andrew Burns**, Head of South Asia Department. Again, this was an extremely busy Department, mainly because of the Civil War that was raging in Sri Lanka between the government and the Liberation Tigers of Tamil Eelam (LTTE) (1983-2009). Because of the time difference, we worked long into the night, but I was happy to do so. I was absorbed so much in what I was doing. It was so interesting, if not a little disturbing at times. Andrew was amazing: kind, calm, considerate. Ideal for the situation. I couldn't have asked for a better boss. Well done again POD!

Time at last for a foreign posting, and so I went to Mexico in October 1987 (the weekend of Michael Fish's famous 'hurricane that never was'). After Mexico it was on to Hungary in 1991, before returning for another home posting in 1994.

Again, I struck exceedingly lucky. I was sent to work as PA to **Anthony Layden**, Head of Western European Department, yet another frantically busy Department, especially when we had to deal with the death of Princess Diana in France, which was very traumatic for us all. Anthony was fantastic (one of my favourites too), and I really liked his wife Josephine, whom I met now and then as they also lived near The Office and invited me to their flat for lunch occasionally. I had cause to be very grateful to Anthony on a few occasions for various personal reasons: the death of dear Dad; the sudden death of my brother-in-law, when I was allowed a few days leave to fly out to Mallorca to stay with my sister who had taken her two sons there immediately afterwards, and who was struggling a great deal; plus other difficult situations I had to deal with.

I stayed with Anthony for five years until The Office offered me Madrid as my next posting. At last! But I knew I couldn't go. Dad had died and Mum missed him dreadfully, as did we all. I had spent so much of my life away from them, and they had sacrificed so much for me, that now it was my turn. Very reluctantly I explained to POD that I couldn't go and asked if I could remain in London until I retired in 2005. They were reluctant to agree, but in the end they did, and from then on it was arranged that I would hold the senior post of PA to the Director (Assistant Under-Secretary of State), Wider Europe for the remainder of my time in London. Again, it was a fascinating, busy job, with the Director being ultimately responsible for Russia and all the *'-stans'*. This was an area of which I knew little, so I learned a lot and very much enjoyed the work.

My Directors (all of whom I liked), came and went. They either retired or went on postings. In turn, I worked for John de Fonblanque, Stephen Wright, John Macgregor and Linda Duffield, but it was John Macgregor whom I liked the best.

It's a small world. John and my sister went to school together and they both played in the Leicestershire Schools Symphony Orchestra (John was a cellist - he now plays the double bass: Sheila is a flautist, as you know). My best friend Marie also went to that school and knows John. She reminded me the other day that when she came to visit me at the FCO and I showed her around, she and John had a good catch-up together. I will never forget either John's kindness to me when Mum died, for which I am so very grateful. He was a great strength during that dreadfully sad time.

I was also thrilled when John put my name forward for an invitation to one of Her Majesty's Garden Parties at Buckingham Palace as a thank you for my work for him. It was such a special, unforgettable, afternoon, which I enjoyed immensely.

After John, for a short time I worked for Linda Duffield. When she went on her posting as Ambassador to the Czech Republic, it was decided to cut her position and streamline the Directorates, thus leaving me without a boss or a job. By now I only had a few months to go until I retired, so it was agreed that I would work for the Head of Whitehall Liaison Department, Clare Smith, until then. This was very handy as the Department was just across the corridor from my own office and I knew and liked Clare, so I stayed where I was, and she moved into Linda's office. I found this work extremely absorbing: the Department 'did what it said on the tin' – it liaised with other parts of Whitehall, but there was one Department in particular, 'up-stream', with whom we had the most contact. And, as icing on the cake, I was thrilled when asked if I would like to pay a familiarization visit to 'the Donut' (as we 'fondly' called GCHQ) – no details, sorry. I jumped at the chance and came away with a much better understanding of some aspects of my work.

It was with tremendous regret, and many tears, that I finally retired from The Office on my 60th birthday, 16 April 2005.

Thank you **so much** to all my Ambassadors for making my career so memorable and happy in so many different ways. For those no longer alive for me to thank, I do so posthumously. But whether still with us or not, I remember you all with affection. Even Charles Wallace, now time has passed. After all, he did have his good points!

Chapter Nine

My Embassy Life and Work

One of the first things Miss Lofting said to me at the very beginning of my career with The Office was:

"Remember Gillian, that you too, as a member of the Diplomatic Service, are an ambassador representing your country abroad".

I have never forgotten her words and have always felt immensely proud to be so. From The Office's point of view, trust, loyalty and integrity were the main attributes I needed. I had access to a great many high security documents and information, and they needed to know I would not divulge any of the knowledge I had, nor betray any confidences. These requirements were always uppermost in my mind, and I stuck to them like glue.

And as the years passed, I also became more and more aware that being an Ambassador's PA at post meant I had a [minor] standing within the Embassy and the wider community. I was the 'gateway to the top', so to speak, and I was conscious that I had to use my position wisely, sensitively and without reproach. No tempting gifts were allowed to be accepted, and any offered had to be reported. It also meant that when dealing with 'matters of the heart', I had to be extra cautious: if any work questions were asked (as in Hungary), I had to report it, and that was the end of that relationship.

The office side of the job

Over the last few years, with the advent of modern technology, the role of a PA has changed almost beyond recognition. Today PAs seem to be more support managers and event planners, serving different bosses and teams. A background in business is more important than a background in a secretarial college, which is where

I learned my skills. However, during my time as an Ambassador's PA, the role was viewed differently, though the qualities needed to be a good PA were the same: efficiency, discretion, an organized mind and excellent communication skills.

In addition, for me, the ability to multitask was vital. There was so much to do and generally so little time to do it. I needed to be well organized, to have patience, and to be able to get on well with others, whether visitors or colleagues. I needed to be flexible (you can say that again!), calm in difficult or dangerous situations (likewise), and compassionate to those around me. I saw some dreadful things during my time abroad and I had to understand.

The practical secretarial side was also important. With no computers, shorthand was a necessity, and with only manual typewriters, good typing skills were essential. We were only given electric typewriters in the early 1980s, progressing on to word processors, with their wrap-around facility, later that decade. Accuracy and speed were always paramount: no deleting, cutting and pasting in those days! PAs now don't know they are born! There were also my cypher duties to perform, as and when required, which called for special skills and concentration.

Added to this was the social side of my job. When there was no Social Secretary, I arranged the Ambassador's social calendar, and that of his wife, involving sending out invitations for receptions and dinner parties, collating the replies, going through the *placement* with them. The Ambassadress (the wife – female Ambassadors are still known as the Ambassador, their partners/husbands as the spouse) usually took charge of the catering side of things and the duties of the Residence staff, but if she needed help, I was there to provide it. So – an extremely busy but satisfying job, it was a very satisfying job, which I loved.

Embassy hours varied depending on the country concerned. We were, and are, of course, open twenty-four hours a day for Consular cases and emergencies, with a Duty Officer and Cypher Officer on call at all times. If only we had had today's mobile phones instead of walkie-talkie radios! We had to carry these great bricks around with us wherever we went during our duty week, and we couldn't stray too far because the reception was poor.

Generally, we started at 0830 and finished at 1700. Mexico City was different: On two days we worked from 0730 straight through to 1430 without a break (I took sandwiches), and for three days we worked from 0830 to 1300, and 1430 to 1700. This took a bit of getting used to, but it was nice to finish early on a Friday so that we could get away for the weekend.

I worked to a set routine: into the Embassy early so that I could go through the Ambassador's diary for that day, coordinating it with mine, noting any visitors or outside calls he had to make; and when he arrived, we checked it together.

I then prepared for any visitors, making sure refreshments were ready for when they arrived. However, when I was working for the Director in London and a foreign Ambassador came in for a dressing down, he got nothing – just to emphasize the gravity of the meeting.

Next came the mail. All the Embassy bags of mail went first to Information Section, who sorted through them and sent the contents to the relevant Sections. Classified mail, of course, arrived in the Diplomatic Bags and went straight up to Chancery, where it was sorted by the Grade 10 Registry Clerk.

All the mail addressed to the Ambassador, both classified and unclassified, came to me. I went through it, setting aside anything I could deal with myself, and took the remainder in to him. He read it and dictated any urgent replies. Once that was done, we spent our day welcoming visitors and dealing with whatever occurred, as and when it did so.

The highlight (?) of my year was THE ANNUAL REVIEW. This was a Head of Mission's summing-up despatch of all that had occurred during the past year, and it went straight to the Foreign Secretary. It was his/her chance to shine and shine they did. Radiance oozed from every pore! In true Sir Humphrey mode, they waxed lyrical. In my case, page after page kept landing on my desk, and it required a great deal of stamina and patience on my part to keep up. What made matters worse was that it was typed on Ambassadorial blue airletter paper, with usually seven carbon copies on the same paper. It was a true nightmare to make corrections, so I had to be accurate. If the mistake wasn't mine, steam came out my ears and I felt like ripping the whole thing up!

Just to clarify. Only the Foreign Secretary, Heads of Mission, Directors, and Heads of Department were allowed to use blue notepaper (airmail or thick blue). Anything that arrived on blue denoted importance and needed immediate attention. And only the Foreign Secretary was allowed to make corrections and comments in red, which usually sent the recipient into a flat spin.

When I first started in The Office, there was no set limit to the length of this Review. However, in the end I think even the Foreign Secretary got a bit fed up with all this paperwork arriving from Heads of Mission throughout the world, and a word limit was stipulated. This then meant, of course, that I had to count it all, and it required a lot of juggling around with the text to make what the Ambassador deemed essential information fit. Yet more corrections! But we got there in the end, and it was sent back to London, with fingers crossed that it didn't return with red all over it.

In my Embassies, the Annual Review was essential reading for all UK based staff, of course, but I had lived through it all so nothing was completely new to me. However, I still found it extremely enlightening as it reflected the Ambassador's own views and observations on certain events and personalities (some of which I already knew and had listened to many times!). The Review was, of course, highly classified.

Social Obligations

There were certain events which it was obligatory for me, and my UK-based colleagues, to attend. The main one was the QBP, on or as near to 3 June (Her Majesty's Official Birthday) as possible. It was always held on a weekday, never a weekend, and the locally employed staff did not attend as we were celebrating our Sovereign's Coronation. Lists of suggested invitees were drawn up by the Heads of Section, and they and the Ambassador went through them together as it was an important opportunity for contacts to be forged or renewed, and Britain to be showcased. I was also allowed to invite the PAs of other Commonwealth Ambassadors, all of whom I knew already both socially and through work. I always enjoyed these: QBPs. Meeting the businessmen, politicians, influential movers and shakers with whom my Ambassador had contact, was an ideal opportunity for me to put a face to a name, and for them to know to whom they were speaking when they telephoned. These were important occasions, and invitations were much sought after (especially Manila!).

We were also expected to attend some, but not all, of the receptions held by the Ambassador and senior members of the Embassy. I went to everything, mainly because I wanted to, but being single, it was useful for the host to have an extra female! Fine. I didn't mind at all. Same for official dinners. I regularly made up the numbers, or partnered a single male, and got invited back by guests.

It was not obligatory, but I always felt it my duty, to attend the Remembrance Day Service at our Anglican Church, and if there was a Commonwealth War Graves cemetery in the capital, that Service as well. If the cemetery was somewhere else in the country, our Honorary Consul attended, along with any ex-pats living in that area. I thought it important to attend given my own family's experiences of both World Wars. Now I bell-ring for these occasions at my own church.

The Remembrance Day Service held at the Commonwealth War Graves Cemetery outside Budapest. Bleak, and freezing cold.

For me, these social obligations were just part of the job. And, of course, I returned the kind hospitality of my colleagues and ex-pat friends by hosting my own 'mini-functions', usually intimate dinner parties for eight as that was all I had room for at home. Only one near disaster in Manila, when a flaming Christmas pudding exploded, and I almost set fire to the place! Otherwise, my guests seem to have really enjoyed my dinners, so they said.

Health matters

Despite being a 'vaccination pin cushion', it was almost impossible to avoid the various ailments that were prevalent in the countries in which I was living. I did my best to stay healthy (the Ambassador got a bit upset if I wasn't around), but local conditions were not always conducive to this and I succumbed to a whole range of illnesses: typhoid, dysentery, cholera, skin infections, brucellosis (milk fever) caught through eating contaminated yoghurt), nervous exhaustion; and I had a major operation in Mexico.

In Guatemala, because I had been badly bitten by mosquitos on the coastal plain, I spent six days in hospital with suspected malaria. I don't think I was lucid part of the time, being either wrapped in foil or surrounded by ice packs, which was not at all pleasant. I never did find out the outcome because we were expelled and all my notes were lost, but malaria was never definitively diagnosed, and it was thought I may have had a very serious liver and kidney virus instead. In Hungary, if I steered clear of those ticks, and put on loads of mosquito repellent, I managed well!

During all the above, I couldn't have asked for better health care. We had first class private doctors and dentists (constantly monitored by the Medical Department in London) and attended private clinics. I owe my physicians a huge debt of gratitude - Dr Zabalhauregui in Manila; Dr Zapff in Peru; Dr Vicuña in Santiago; and Dr Drijanski (my GP) and Dr Rocha del Valle (my surgeon) in Mexico. I remember you all with great affection. I couldn't have survived as well as I did without you. Thank you.

Diplomatic Bag Runs

For me, in addition to my day-to-day duties, there were a few 'added treats' when the Ambassador was away travelling, and one of them was that I could take my turn on the Diplomatic Bag runs. To save money, the QM didn't call at very small posts unless there was a special reason for him to do so, so we UK based took it in turns to take the Bag up to that Embassy. As you can imagine, these trips were jealously coveted by all concerned.

There were two posts where I did this: **Lima** up to **Laz Paz,** and **Santiago** to **Rio de Janeiro.** No wonder we were loath to give them up!

On the Lima to **La Paz** run, I set off at sea level and reached thirteen thousand feet in two and a half hours. The Bag had to remain with me at all times. If it wasn't too big, I took it to the loo with me, which was sometimes a bit of squash. If it was too big or there was more than one Bag, the Senior Cabin Crew member stood guard over it/them until I got back to my seat. I was always the first off the plane (wonderful!), and a UK based member of staff came in the Embassy car to the aircraft steps to whisk me away through the Diplomatic channel and on to the Embassy. It always worked like clockwork, as it should have done, except in Guatemala.

The main problem for me on this run was *soroche* (altitude sickness). Nearly all of us suffered as the flight time was insufficient to acclimatize ourselves from sea level to such an altitude. I know I did. My colleague from the Embassy brought an oxygen cylinder which I had to use, and from then on, I drank cups of *mate de coca* (an infusion of cocaine leaves, of which there is an abundance in Bolivia, of course) to ease the sickness. It was invaluable and worked a treat (I hasten to add I didn't continue the habit once back at sea level!).

I was in La Paz for two nights, staying in a very nice hotel off the main thoroughfare in the downtown area (the UK based staff lived in a residential district a little lower down, but only just). On the first night, the H of C gave me dinner, which was a great chance to catch on events in Peru and Bolivia, and a little bit of Office gossip.

The next day I had to myself, and I took a tour on each of my two visits, both to Lake Titicaca and the Altiplano. I couldn't get enough of the culture and scenery, even though I felt quite queasy at that altitude: it was a thrilling experience to be there.

A little Uros girl on Suriki Island,   Las Cholitas at Altiplano
one of the man-made floating islands
on Lake Titicaca

It was always a little hair-raising leaving the Altiplano, where the airport was situated. At this altitude the jet engines had great difficulty in taking off through lack of oxygen. We always flew Lufthansa, and each time it took my flight two tries to get off the ground. On the third try we were airborne – time for a stiff drink, I always felt!

When in Santiago, I made two Bag runs to **Rio de Janeiro**. The Brazilian seat of Government moved from Rio to Brasilia in 1960 and for a time Britain operated two Embassies: one in Brasilia during the winter months, one in Rio during the summer. However, the Embassy moved completely to Brasilia in 1972 and the Rio office was downgraded to a consulate general.

It seemed more economical for the QM to deliver Rio's classified consular documents, passports etc. to us in Santiago, for onward transmission to Rio, which was the main tourist hub. We never complained! This gave us a chance to escape living under martial law for two nights, which was very much anticipated and appreciated.

Again, I stayed in a nice hotel near the consulate general, and during the free day I took tours around this beguiling city, but not before I had been given a briefing by the consulate staff on security. I should wear no jewellery; take little cash (I had no credit cards); not walk alone off the main roads; not go out on my own from the hotel in the evenings. This was why I went on the tours. Fortunately, in the time I had, I managed to visit the popular attractions, and really enjoyed the atmosphere of the city.

'North of the Border, San Antonio Way'!

Another exciting (for me) 'treat' came when I was in Mexico. The Embassy bought our official cars, tax free, from San Antonio in Texas, which was much cheaper. We needed a new car, and the question was: how to get it to Mexico City? As I love driving, I volunteered to drive it down as the Ambassador was away travelling for a week. The Admin Officer jumped at the chance, and as luck would have it our newly arrived Second Secretary Commercial, Roger, and wife Gill, had also just bought their car from the same dealership, so we could travel together. It was decided we would fly up to San Antonio; spend two nights there sorting out all the paperwork; cross the US border at Laredo; drive to Monterrey, where we would spend one night; on to Zacatecas, another night there; then back to Mexico City. I would drive the Embassy saloon, and Roger and Gill would drive their estate car, joining me now and then to give me a break.

We left the DF on the evening flight, checked into our hotel in San Antonio, and arrived early next morning at the dealership to complete the formalities. This done, there was time to visit *The Alamo*, which I had always wanted to see (it's much smaller than I had imagined) and do a bit more sightseeing around the River Walk before returning to the hotel for an early night as we had a long journey south the next day.

We set off at 7 am to drive the 176 miles to the US border at Laredo. When we got to the crossing, it was heaving, but we passed though the Diplomatic Channel with no problems. On then a further 140 miles to **Monterrey**, along the longest, straightest and almost deserted road I have ever come across, with only cacti for company. We drove in a close convoy – just in case.

The long and lonely road to Monterrey!

It was another early start the next day. Having been told by the dealer that there were few filling stations on our route south, and that they were very far apart, the first thing we had to do before leaving Monterrey was to buy spare cans of petrol. This we did, and after a bit of trouble finding our way out of the city, we eventually began our 287-mile journey to Zacatecas. Now and then Gill or Roger would join me, either to drive a bit, or just keep me company. We had our fingers crossed as these were new cars and we were running them in, so any breakdowns in the desert would have been a real headache. It did seem a long way - same old Joshua trees, cactus, dust and emptiness - through what is, today, drug baron country. I would hate to have been ambushed in such a remote part of the country. Nowadays, there are *autopistas,* so the journey wouldn't be so arduous or dangerous, but we back then were always on the lookout for trouble.

At last, we arrived at **Zacatecas, f**ounded in 1546 after silver deposits were discovered in the area. It is a picturesque colonial town lying in a valley surrounded by steep hills. Its streets are narrow, with many impressive Baroque limestone buildings adding to its character. We were so pleased to stretch our legs and wander around, but we didn't have the energy to walk too far afield. However, we saw the most important buildings, like the stunning Cathedral and the *Palacio de Gobierno* (town hall).

The Palacio de Gobierno

We had an even earlier start the next day (we were getting used to this) as it was 382 miles to the DF, climbing all the way up to 7000 feet at which the capital lies. At times the cars struggled a bit, and so did I coping with mild *soroche,* though when living in Mexico City it never seemed to bother me. We kept going, stopping infrequently, and at last, by late evening, we arrived back at the Embassy, deposited the cars there and headed home. I must say I was exhausted and slept most of the next day, but it had been an unforgettable experience. I had seen parts of Mexico that I would never have visited otherwise and learned a lot about the history and geography of the regions we had passed through along the way.

The Ambassador was most interested to hear my account of the journey and was pleased that I had taken the initiative and helped in this way. My pleasure, Ambassador. Delighted to be of service!

Trials and Tribulations
As I'm sure anyone living abroad will tell you, various things are sent to try us - often. We, in our Embassies, were lucky as we always had

a 'Mr Fixit', a locally employed member of the Admin Section who knew his way around the 'systems' (sometimes dubious) of the various countries in which we were posted.

However, there were times when the Section was so busy that we were left to sort out our own administrative matters, with varying degrees of success.

One particular occasion springs to mind. I had arrived in Mexico in October 1987, and by Christmas I was still living on the minimal *float* as my baggage had not put in an appearance. This was driving me mad so, with Admin's blessing, I decided to go to the Mexican Customs depot to look for it myself over the Christmas break.

When I turned up on 28 December, I wasn't feeling all that well as I had been hit in the face by an exploding Christmas pudding (yet another one) on Christmas Day, which had necessitated a trip to the hospital, lots of ointment and a temporary eye patch. But not even that was going to stop me getting my baggage, so I presented myself at the Customs Office, sheaf of papers in hand, and enquired where my crates were.

Despite my visas and other pieces of evidence, I had a hard time convincing the officials that I was in fact one of the diplomatic staff working at the British Embassy, but after nearly three hours of to-ing and fro-ing and wrangling, it was finally decided that my paperwork was in fact in order, and yes, my crates were here: I could go and collect them. Fantastic!

How was I to do this? First, I was told I had to find a forklift truck and agree how much it would cost. I located one, but when the driver knew the Embassy was paying, cash registers danced in front of his eyes, and he quoted an extortionate amount. There then followed more haggling (in Spanish of course), and I was finally able to reduce the price, but not by much unfortunately: the Embassy would have to sort that one out. How I longed for Mr Fixit!

Following my forklift truck driver, I weaved my way through machinery, timber, other crates and containers, no small feat with only one eye, until, alleluia, I saw two large crates, upside down, with ANGRAVE stamped on them. "Where is the lorry?" the driver asked. Lorry? What lorry? I thought you dealt with all that. Certainly not. So off I went again in search of a lorry. I had now spent nearly all day, with no lunch, wandering around these yards, and I was getting thoroughly fed up to say the least. I was inundated with offers (mostly of lorries, but not all!), yet more cash registers before their eyes, no doubt. Eventually I chose a quiet young man who had been elbowed out of the way by the older, more pushy ones, and off we went back to the loading bay to collect my crates.

The forklift truck driver then proceeded to put the fork right through one of the crates, with a great tinkling sound. There goes my television and beautiful Noritake dinner service, I thought, and I was right. Could I get compensation? No chance (though the insurance did pay in the end!)

At last, I set off back home, with the lorry driver following, and with dear Cándido's help, the crates were opened, and the boxes offloaded. Finally! What a relief. I collapsed in a heap and had a large glass of wine to celebrate. This was the best Christmas present ever.

I don't believe it!   (Cándido far right)

After that, apart from Guatemala, where I never did get my car because we were expelled before the paperwork was completed, I left everything to Admin Section and became resigned to any minor inconveniences or delays. It was much better for my blood pressure that way.

Embassy life was definitely for me. I thrived on it, even the hard work and long hours. I always felt I was part of a team, and I took great pride in what I was doing, and whom I was representing. I think this showed in the valedictory letter I received from David Warren. To receive such accolades, and to know that others felt I had made an important contribution too, made it all worthwhile.

Chapter Ten

Official Visitors

A large and important part of an Embassy's time is dedicated to visitors – Royalty, politicians, businessmen, show biz personalities. The list is endless and, whilst they raised the profile of the Embassy, they also caused me a lot of work. Not that I minded: at least I got to meet them, albeit briefly some of the time. For me, the most memorable occasions were:

The State Visit to Hungary, 4-7 May 1993
This was by far the most important visit I was involved in. I was frazzled at the end of it!

With the fall of Communism, it seemed everyone wanted to visit Hungary, and Her Majesty The Queen and HRH The Duke of Edinburgh were no exception. The liaison with the Palace began at least a year before the actual date of the visit, with attention to detail at every stage. Nothing was left to chance. Even comfort stops were timed. The itinerary was rehearsed many times; security checked constantly; certain venues were spruced up by the Hungarian Government; the guest lists for receptions and dinners minutely scrutinized. It went on and on, and into overdrive six months before the actual date. And in between all this planning, the day-to-day running of the Embassy had to continue. So, it meant many late hours for us all, me included.

The Visit was a tremendous success. Her Majesty and HRH were welcomed warmly by President Arpad Göncz, the Prime Minister, and other senior Hungarian officials. They were staying as guests of the Hungarian Government at the Government Guest House, so at least their accommodation was taken care of, and the Ambassador didn't have to worry on that score.

It was a landmark occasion, also, when Her Majesty was asked to address the Hungarian Parliament, the first time ever that a member of the Royal Family had been asked to do so. I was very privileged to be invited to attend that Address.

Her Majesty addressing
The Hungarian Parliament
(I am far right in the balcony)

Enjoying a display of horsemanship
at Bugacz

There were various trips away from Budapest, and of course many receptions and a State dinner. And on the day they were due to leave, I was thrilled to have been selected, because of all the work I had done for their Visit, as one of the Embassy staff to have a private audience with them. (No photographs were allowed.)

I had been well briefed as to what to do, but when the time came, I was very nervous. I'd been practicing my curtseys like mad, making sure my hat didn't fall off. We had to wear gloves as well and trying to find a suitable hat and gloves in Hungary when there were no shops, had been a real problem, but eventually I had done so.

The Equerry called my name, and I went into the salon alone, walking along a red carpet to the end of the long room where Her Majesty and HRH were standing. I curtseyed; Her Majesty held out her hand (I was not to offer mine first) and I shook it: same with HRH.

"Thank you so much for all the hard work you have done for our Visit," Her Majesty said. "I hope you will be able to have the chance of a break." Her Majesty then presented me with a signed photograph of them both.

"It's been a great privilege to have done so, Ma'am", I replied, nodding to HRH too. Then it was for me to make the next remark.

"Actually, I'm driving home tomorrow for a few days leave."

"You're driving?", asked The Duke. "Yes, Sir." "How long will that take you?". "Two and a half days, Sir."

At which point The Duke turned to Her Majesty and said: "There you are. I told you it was too far to bring the horses." I nodded wisely, not having the faintest clue as to how horses travel. Another "Thank you". I curtseyed, the Equerry appeared and off I went, clutching my prized photograph.

The Ambassador saying farewell to Her Majesty and the Duke of Edinburgh

And as I've said before, we were so proud when the Ambassador received his Knighthood, in private, at the end of the Visit. So justly deserved for both he and his wife.

Other Royals

Budapest: My Ambassador John Birch meeting Princess Diana

Hungary seemed to be the main destination for other members of the Royal Family, and there seemed to be quite a few of them: HRH Princess Diana and HRH Prince [King] Charles (separately). Prince Charles had a very busy itinerary, but he engaged so well with all those he met, mainly members of the business community, and his visit was invaluable to us. During the reception we held for him at the Embassy, I had to escort him up to the Ambassador's private 'facility' when it was needed, praying that I wouldn't forget the combination to get into Chancery. I really liked him, and he was easy to talk to. Then there was the Duke of Kent, Princess Michael of Kent (often, I escorted her to the airport each time), and Prince Andrew.

Prince Andrew came out in October 1992 as a member of the Defence Staff College_Delegation and wished to play golf (as he did). Since I was the only member of the Embassy to play seriously, the Ambassador asked if I would take him to the course at Szentendre for a round, which I did. Dave Hart, our Security Officer, had played a little bit, so he came too.

Dave and I played against HRH and a very nice Delegation member, called Alistair. The Detective came along for the walk, and Hungarian Boris was never far behind.

It didn't start well. I was so nervous I shanked my first two drives into the woods. HRH's eyes rolled to the top of his head. This is going to be a push-over. A few words of encouragement from the Detective, a hug from Alistair, and I drove off again. It was a cracking shot (I wasn't 1991 Hungarian Ladies Open champion for nothing!). After that, I just couldn't put a foot or shot wrong, and we won. I must say HRH was very magnanimous in defeat, but I realized I could say goodbye to any hope of a Damehood or early retirement.

He invited me to dinner that evening with some of the other Delegates. I didn't feel I could refuse! This didn't start well either, as HRH started to tell some very rude stories, which made me feel most uncomfortable, so much so that in the end the other Delegates told him to stop, which he did. After that, all went well, although at the end, when I said I would drop Alistair off at the place where they were staying, leaving HRH to return to the Residence, where he was staying, he made some unnecessary and suggestive remarks which I didn't like, but I made no comment.

I said nothing to the Ambassador about this when I returned to the Embassy. However, Prince Andrew's visit came up in conversation when I met him and Prim for lunch at the end of 2019, a few months before he died, and I told him then. He was horrified and asked why I hadn't let him know at the time. I said I didn't want to cause any trouble, and what could he have done anyway? But he said that didn't matter: he would have wanted to know anyway. He was so sorry. But that is all in the past now and, after a few more 'observations' on the visit, in the end we had a good laugh about it.

Dave Hart, HRH, Danny Haynal (owner of the golf club) and me.

Visiting Politicians, VIPs and Entertainers
As I said, in Mexico we had been fortunate to host HRH The Duke of Edinburgh, as well as captains of industry.

But my very favourite visitor had to be Sir David Attenborough who came twice to see the Monarch butterflies. These fragile little black and red insects start their annual migration from the northern parts of North America in early autumn, and fly about one hundred and ninety miles a day until they reach the *Oyamel* fir forests in Central Mexico. Here they settle in huge clusters in the trees until Spring, when they mate and head off north again on their epic journey. The females lay about five hundred eggs, and then sadly die. I have been to these forests, and it is a truly amazing spectacle to see them.

Sir David and I both come from Leicester, so we had a good chat about home. But I also told him I felt an affinity with these butterflies as I too, flew great distances, settled, missed out the mating bit, and then was off again. He roared with laughter and said he could just imagine how I felt. He did the same too, at times.

In Peru, Cecil Parkinson came out on an official visit, but it was to Hungary that most of the politicians, VIPs and entertainers flocked, not only because of the change in the political situation there, but also because it was near.

Again, a favourite visitor of mine was Prime Minister **John Major** who, 5 December 1994, along with Douglas Hurd as Foreign Secretary, visited Budapest for the OSCE Conference, with special emphasis on war-torn Bosnia. He was charming. I well remember frantically trying to finish typing his Press Statement when I felt an arm around my shoulders. I was about to shrug it off when I looked up and it was John Major. "I just wanted to thank you for all your hard work for our visit", he said, which I thought was exceedingly kind of him to take the trouble to say so. We had a brief exchange, and I went back to pounding the keyboard. But I never forgot those words. A 'thank you' makes so much difference.

Then there was **Ted Heath**, who visited us when he was Father of the House. He agreed to chat to us UK based staff in our secure Chancery area. Our DA asked if there was anything he would have done differently during his term as Prime Minister, and in politics in general. Without any hesitation, he replied testily that he would have appointed a different Secretary of Education (a refence to Margaret Thatcher). Speaking about it together afterwards, we all agreed that it spoke volumes about his dislike of Mrs. Thatcher, and his bitterness at having been 'deposed' by her as Leader of the Conservative Party.

As Madame Speaker (the first woman ever to have held that position), **Betty Boothroyd** also paid us a visit. She was fantastic: elegant, amusing, though quite particular. Great 'value for money', and the Hungarians liked her.

On the entertainment side we, and the British Council mainly, also welcomed John Nettles (who performed the soliloquy from 'Twelfth Night' at the famous art-deco hotel, the New York Palace; and Rod

Stewart. (I also was fortunate enough to see the Three Tenors, though we weren't involved in their visit.)

There were, of course, many more important visitors to our Embassies, far too many, I fear, to recount them all. But a great deal was achieved, both commercially and politically, from their visits and our meetings with those who came, which was exceedingly satisfying all round.

PART SIX

Unrest, Dispute and Civil War, Conflict, and Peacekeeping

Chapter Eleven

Unrest

For some reason, from the moment I joined The Office, Personnel seemed to think that countries that were experiencing unrest, civil wars, disputes or conflicts was just what I needed. Whether they thought I would work well in these environments (which I did) or, being an older entrant, I would cope better, who knows? But this seemed to be my lot.

The Philippines

My first posting was to the Philippines which, when I arrived in October 1976, had been placed under martial law by President Ferdinand Marcos since 23 September 1972. His pretext for doing so was in response to the 'communist threat' then posed by the newly formed CCP (Communist Party of the Philippines), and the rebellion of the MIM (Mindanao Independence Movement) in the southern island of Mindanao.

Marcos was accused by his opponents of exaggerating the threat and using martial law as a convenient excuse to consolidate his power and extend his term of office beyond the two Presidential terms as set out in the 1935 constitution. Once he was ousted, it was also discovered that this had also allowed him, and his wife Imelda (of shoe fame) to stash away large amounts of money gained through illegal means.

During the day, this didn't bother me much (nor my colleagues). There were certain areas particularly in downtown Manila, where we were advised not to go because of the risk of muggings. Otherwise, I was free to travel where I wanted (but not to Mindanao), and I did, often alone, or with Ann the Ambassador's PA, or my good friend Pam who came out to visit me. We experienced no problems and felt quite safe. The main danger was the lunatic drivers!

But we were all subject to a curfew from midnight till 0500, which was inconvenient to say the least, and a real pain when we were on duty for a week at a time and frequently had to go into the Embassy out of office hours. This was normally to send or receive urgent telegrams to and from London where, because of the time difference, they did not work the same hours as us. All very irritating, but an important part of the job!

Peru

I was ecstatic when I learned that my next posting was to be to Peru. I'd wanted to go to South American for so long, and now I was actually going. Well done, Personnel. At this rate we are destined to have a long and happy future together!

I took up my posting in Peru at the beginning of 1980, just before Fernando Bélaunde Terry was sworn in as the new, democratically elected, President. He had previously been the country's President from 1963-1968 but was ousted in a military coup.

When I arrived, the country's economy was in deep recession and there was the prospect of civil unrest, so the ruling military administration, to forestall this, allowed an election for the restoration of constitutional rule. Bélaunde won a five-year term, receiving forty-five per cent of the vote in a fifteen-man contest.

He then set about carrying out many much-needed popular reforms, including great improvements to Peru's infrastructure by the building of a highway linking Chiclayo, on the Pacific coast, to the isolated Amazon region.

The situation stabilized and, whilst there were still armed soldiers on the streets, they were not in great evidence, and we were allowed to carry on our daily lives without any problem.

However, there was one big cloud on the horizon: an ever-growing group of leftist insurgents, namely the *Sendero Luminoso* (Shining

Path) under the control of the former university professor, Abimael Guzman. They were vicious and earned the reputation of one of the most ruthless terrorist groups in the Western Hemisphere. When I was there, they terrorized the population in the rural and mountainous areas, carrying out assassinations, bombing raids and ambushes, so there were definite parts of the country that we were forbidden to visit. This was a shame as the Andean villages were fascinating and places I certainly wanted to see. But it wasn't safe to go there, so that was that.

They are still active today, though they have turned to drug-trafficking to fund their activities and are now trying to convert the population to their Maoist ideals by peaceful indoctrination rather than violence.

Guatemala

As you'll read in my next Chapter, Guatemala was not an easy posting for we British over Belize. When I was there it wasn't much fun to live in that country anyway because of the civil war that had been raging since 1960. Such a shame as there was so much to see and do, but as the main focus of the insurgency and violence occurred in the rural areas, it just wasn't safe to travel far afield because of the risk of kidnap and ransom.

In Guatemala City itself, the atmosphere was tense. Repression occurred on a daily basis, especially of government opponents and critics, left-wing academics and politicians. There were certain places where bodies were routinely dumped, as I discovered to my horror on one occasion. You soon learned where the no-go parts of the city were, and political discussion of any kind was definitely to be avoided at all costs. Of course, the military were out in force, their guns much in evidence, though that didn't bother me much as I'd seen it all before. I came to expect it to a certain degree.

Yet again there was a very strict curfew in place, which ruled out any late-night visits to restaurants, theatres or cinemas, though I did manage to get tickets to a wonderful early evening *marimba* (Guatemala's national instrument, a bit like a xylophone) concert.

In the modern residential suburbs where we lived, we were more or less free to go where we wanted for shopping and eating out, but I rarely ventured into the old part of the city as, being tall, blonde and obviously foreign, I just didn't feel safe. Kidnapping, sadly, was fairly common in that country.

As you will read, it all went horribly wrong at the end, so my memories of Guatemala are not of the best, sad to say.

Chile

What a surprise. Martial Law yet again. It seemed as if I had been carrying that placard around my neck forever. As you will read from my Chapter on the Falklands, when I arrived in Chile in February 1982, the country was in the hands of the dictator, Augusto Pinochet, who had justified seizing power from President Salvador Allende in a military coup on 11 September 1976 because of the economic crisis and breakdown of democracy that had occurred during his Presidency.

Dissidents were persecuted and political parties suppressed. Over three thousand opponents to the régime were missing, *'los desaparecidos'* (the 'disappeared'), amongst whom was William Beausire, a British stockbroker with dual British and Chilean nationality, who was abducted while in transit in Buenos Aires airport in November 1974, taken to a torture centre in Chile and never seen again. Much of our time in Chancery was spent trying to find out where he was and what had happened to him, but we never did so, despite the mountain of information we amassed.

Also, the Embassy was very much involved prior to my arrival in the case of the British subject Dr Sheila Cassidy, who had been arrested in 1975 for treating Nelson Gutierrez, an opponent of Pinochet, and had been taken to the notorious Villa Grimaldi, where she had been severely tortured. She was subsequently released and returned to the UK through UK Government intervention, in which the Embassy played an important part. She then went on to campaign against the human rights abuses that were happening in Chile at that time.

So, the situation in that country was not ideal either.

But on a day-to-day basis, being British and a member of the Embassy, I led a more or less normal life, going out and about, socializing, joining the Prince of Wales Country Club where I played my tennis, golf and hockey to my heart's content. I was free to travel, which I did as extensively as my leave would allow, and my great friend Pam came out to visit twice (more of our travels together later). The only restriction was the curfew, and a few areas where you did not go.

Despite the political situation, Chile has to be my favourite posting.

Mexico

By the time I arrived in Mexico in October 1987 (the weekend of Michael Fish's 'hurricane that never was'), I was becoming inured to the situation in my new country of residence being not quite what I would have wished for. This was the time of the **Mexican Dirty War** which was an internal conflict running from the 1969s to the 1980s between the ruling PRI Party (*Partido Revolucionario Institucional*), backed by the US Government, and left-wing student and *guerrilla* groups. Again, there were *'desaparecidos'*, torture and most likely executions of those in opposition to the PRI.

The situation got slightly better on 1 December 1988 when a general election was held and the PRI candidate, Carlos Salinas de Gortari, was elected, though of course there were accusations of electoral fraud. He was an economist and so most of the focus turned to trade. The economic situation improved, free trade was at the forefront of his political policies, and the country began to modernize. And the Americans liked him, which helped!

However, from a personal safety point of view, Mexico was somewhat lawless. I was mugged twice (outside the Embassy, which I felt was a bit much), once being lucky not to have my arm ripped off as a passenger in a car leaned out of the window and grabbed my bag with the strap wrapped round my arm for safety. That didn't work! Pickpockets were also an everyday feature when walking around, so you soon learned to be alert wherever you went.

Despite all that, though, I loved my time in Mexico too, and have very fond memories of that country, recounted later.

Hungary

I hadn't wanted to go to Hungary. In fact, I couldn't believe it when I opened the envelope in Mexico City and found that was to be my next posting. Surely not. I was quite settled in South America. But that was the trouble: there was a danger I was 'going native', something The Office definitely discouraged, despite the experience it offered. Time to move on to pastures new, Gillian.

However, looking on the bright side, at least there was no martial law, conflict or unrest, but when I arrived in March 1991 it was just at the end of Communism and Hungary was facing a different challenge. The first free parliamentary election had been held in May 1990 and a new coalition under Prime Minister Jozsef Antall was formed between the Hungarian Democratic Forum (MDF) and the Christian Democrats People's Party. The Russian troops had begun their withdrawal, finally leaving on 19 June 1991. Hungary's future looked bright.

However, without the stability and security that the Communist years had brought, living standards began to decline as a new market economy developed. Prices rose, unemployment soared as the unprofitable smoke-stack industries closed, and inflation reached thirty-five per cent.

As inevitably happens in such a situation, when day to day living standards deteriorate, the governing party starts to become unpopular, and this is what happened to the coalition. New elections were to be held in 1994, but it was difficult to see how a new government could improve matters.

However, when I arrived, things seemed fairly peaceful. Prices were high, but there was little to buy in the shops anyway. I did find the workforce extremely rude and xenophobic, having been unused to foreigners for so long. Visiting your local *csemege* (*csem* for short), the nearest thing there was to a mini supermarket, was a bruising experience, both mentally and physically. I felt I'd been attacked by a band of marauding Huns, and if I managed to escape with what I had gone in there for, I was lucky. To add to this feeling of being the enemy, it took me a long time to be accepted by my neighbours, who were resentful of a single female owning a new car (my Escort, bought with another FCO car loan), and living in a largish flat on her own. But we got there in the end, and we were good friends by the time I left.

The last vestiges of Communism

The Memento Park, Budapest

Romania. A departing Russian tank

I was able to travel fairly extensively on my own in Hungary with no problem, despite not speaking Hungarian well at all. This was not true of Serbia and Romania, though, where I had to travel in a group, and we encountered a good deal of suspicion and antagonism.

But by the time I left Budapest in 1994, I was grateful for the opportunity this posting had afforded me of broadening my horizons by living in a completely different environment to the one I had been used to. So perhaps The Office was right in sending me there after all!

Chapter Twelve

Dispute and Civil War – Guatemala

A Brief History

Like so many other South American countries, Guatemala is no stranger to a troubled past. For you to understand what it was like living there in 1981, I think it's important to know a bit about the country's chequered history.

Its ancient origins began with the Mayan civilization (330 BC – 250 AD), of which the ruins of *Tikal* are a fascinating legacy, but its modern history can be traced back to the arrival in 1525 of the Spanish *Conquistador,* Pedro de Alvarado ('The Invader' as the Mayans called him), who immediately set about subjugating the indigenous population and creating the Captaincy General of Guatemala, which lasted for almost three hundred and thirty years. Initially, this Captaincy included, in addition to Guatemala, what is now the State of Chiapas in Mexico, El Salvador, Nicaragua, Honduras and Costa Rica. Guatemala became independent from the Captaincy in 1821 and was then incorporated in the First Mexican Empire until 1823. From 1824 it was part of the Federal Republic of Central America, and when the Republic was dissolved in 1841, Guatemala became fully independent.

Guatemala is a very fertile country, and in the late 19th century and early 20th centuries she attracted many foreign agricultural companies such as the United Fruit Company (UFC) who were protected and supported by its authoritarian rulers. The United States government in particular supported the savage labour regulations and the massive concessions granted to wealthy landowners. Unsurprisingly, this led to civilian unrest, culminating in 1944 in a popular uprising which heralded the start of the ten-year Guatemalan Revolution.

During this time, the two Presidents, Juan Jose Arevalo and Jacobo Arbenz, instigated social and economic reforms which disadvantaged the UFC, eventually leading it to lobby the United States government to overthrow these reformist governments and install military regimes. The resultant coup took place in 1954 which ended the Guatemalan Revolution. There then followed successive repressive military governments which in turn started the civil war that lasted from 1960 to 1996. At the end of the war in 1997, Guatemala re-established a representative democratic government, but has struggled ever since to enforce the rule of law. To date there is still a very high rate of crime and continued extrajudicial killings , often committed by the security forces.

Belize

It is also important to understand the dispute between Great Britain and Guatemala over Belize.

In 1788 Spain granted Great Britain permission to settle in the area that is today known as Belize, whilst retaining sovereignty. Britain then assumed control when the Spanish Empire was dismantled in 1816, and in 1859 signed a treaty with Guatemala delineating the borders. The area was then renamed British Honduras and it became a Crown Colony in 1862. In 1933 Guatemala lodged a claim that Britain had reneged on one of the provisions in the 1859 Treaty, which thereby nullified it. Guatemala then claimed sovereignty itself as the legal heir to the Spanish Empire. British Honduras voted to remain under our protection but with a greater degree of autonomy, resulting in Guatemala closing its borders with British Honduras in 1948 and severing diplomatic relations with us in 1963. In 1964 we granted British Honduras self-government, but we continued to have a military presence there. The country was renamed Belize in 1976.

Britain took the case to the UN and in 1980 the UN General Assembly adopted the Belizean Independence Resolution by a 125:1 majority, Guatemala being against, unsurprisingly. The Assembly then demanded that Guatemala enter into negotiations with us over

Belize, which they refused to do. There followed widespread local unrest, and negotiations broke down completely, resulting in the closure of our Consulate-General and we UK based staff (me included) being expelled from the country on 12 September 1981 (how can I forget). Britain and Belize agreed on a Constitution and Independence was formally granted on 22 September 1981.

My Arrival

It was into this unstable and perilous environment that I stepped off the plane at La Aurora International Airport in May 1981. I was not in too good a state myself, both mentally and physically, after my early, unplanned departure from Peru, but I was determined to make the most of my new posting. I arrived at the Consulate-General full of optimism, with high hopes of getting out and about and seeing as much of this beautiful country as I could.

How wrong I was! Because of the ongoing tensions between us and Guatemala over Belize, we British were not at all popular, and this for me became the most traumatic posting of my diplomatic career. My time in Guatemala was both dangerous and distressing, and some of the events that happened then come back to haunt me to this day. Whoever thought that diplomatic life revolves around receptions and Ferrero Rocher, think again. I can assure you that it doesn't!

Living conditions were difficult because of the civil war, and on two occasions I saw bodies that had been thrown into the *barranca* near to where I lived. There were military personnel everywhere, armed to the hilt, but having lived through martial law in the Philippines, and with Peru only just becoming a democratic nation, this was for me a regular sight and I accepted it without question.

Because of the political situation, it meant also that we were not free to travel. I longed to visit the impressive Mayan pyramids at *Tikal*, and the famous market at Chichicastenango, but we were ideal targets for kidnap (these happened very often) and so we were limited to travelling with a twenty mile radius of Guatemala City, and then only in groups. However, I did manage to visit **La Democracia**, on the tropical plain (where I got bitten to death my mosquitos), **Antigua** and **Lake Amatitlán** where Chris, one or our UK based, had rented a boat for the duration.

My saving grace was my colleagues. We were seven UK based, including two married couples and two children aged five and seven. In addition, there were fifteen fantastic locally employed. My boss, as you will have read, was the most charming man, Michael Wilmshurst. I was his PA, but because we were a mini-Mission, I helped out generally with a range of other tasks, including cypher duties and accompanying the Queen's Messenger to the airport with the Diplomatic Bags.

Life was ticking along, when all of a sudden, all hell broke loose.

Our Expulsion – 12 September 1981

Having just spent six days in a private clinic with suspected malaria, I had only been back at work three days when, because of the breakdown of talks between Great Britain and Guatemala over the imminent Independence of Belize, Michael was summoned to a meeting with the Foreign Minister, a fairly regular occurrence so we weren't too worried.

When he came back, he was ashen.

"Gill, could you please ask all the UK based to come to my office immediately", he asked.

This I did, and it was then that he told us that Guatemala had broken off diplomatic relations with Great Britain and we were all being expelled from the country. The Consulate-General was being shut down and the locally employed dismissed. And we had just three days to do all this as we were to leave the country on 11 September. It was arranged that the Swiss Embassy, being neutral, would look after our affairs under their Interests Section, for which we paid them;

and one UK based could stay on for a few more days to help them sort out our leases, sell cars, arrange onward transmission of our baggage, and tie up all the loose ends.

I remember we just stood there in stunned silence. Neither Michael, nor any of us, had expected such a drastic outcome. He then asked me to get all the locally employed together as he wanted to tell them on his own. When he returned to his office, he was visibly extremely upset. I made him a coffee, shut the door, and left him until he felt he could face us again.

We also learned that a bomb had just been detonated outside our new Consulate-General building, blowing out all the windows. Whether the perpetrator(s) thought we had moved in already, we don't know. Just as well for us that we hadn't.

The next three days were a nightmare. There was so much to do: files and equipment to be destroyed or bagged up; commercial and other contacts to be informed; Consular cases to be handed over to the Swiss; the locally employed to be looked after as they searched for other employment; and our own affairs to be sorted out. The list was never ending, and the cypher machine and shredder almost caught fire through overuse.

And everything had to be done 'by the book', which meant we were almost glued to our beloved DSP (Diplomatic Service Procedure), all twenty-one volumes of it! It was taking so long to wade through it, that in frustration Michael asked me to send a message to London saying '"For goodness sake stop quoting DSP. We don't have time to look it up. You do it, and just give us the answer."

This seemed to work a treat, and we got on much faster after that.

Thinking outside the box became our mantra, and on occasions I had some rather odd tasks to perform, like trying to burn secret files in a brazier at the end of the Residence garden at 1 am with the rain pouring down. I wasn't too successful, and ended up having to bag up the charred remains for the QM to take back with him.

My most frightening moment came late in the evening on the second day. Michael had asked me to collect some urgent, important documents from an office in downtown Guatemala City. I had to take the official car, not ideal as it was easily identifiable by the number plates, but we had no choice. I collected the papers and was just returning to the dark empty car park when a soldier who had been paying me unwanted attention suddenly grabbed me and pushed me up against a well. He held the bayonet of his rifle against my throat and with great venom started to harangue me over Belize, Britain, we in the Consulate – anything he could think of connected to us. I was petrified, and really thought he would shoot me there and then. After all, in a Civil war, what is one more body. I had visions of being just another statistic found in a *barranca* somewhere. I don't know how long this lasted, but it seemed like an eternity. I just stood there quietly, looking at the floor. Eventually he took the bayonet away from my throat, motioned for me to get in our car, but gave me an almighty push as I was doing so, which sent me sprawling. It really hurt, but he just stood there jeering. I struggled to my feet, got into the car, locked the door and drove off like a bat from hell, but not before I saw him in my rear view mirror waving his rifle at me. I expected a bullet through the window at any moment, but to my great relief none came.

When I got back to the office, I was shaking all over. Michael was horrified and furious. We talked it through, but he had enough on his plate and any representation by him would have been counter-productive, so we agreed to leave it. But he raised the matter when he got back to London. I can never forget that encounter. I can see that soldier's horrible face to this day.

The Silver Greyhound
On the third day our marvellous QM, Jim Hollis, a good friend of mine, arrived at the Consulate to take the Diplomatic Bags back to

London, all three hundred kilos of them. With Gordon, our Admin Officer, I was tasked with accompanying him to the airport to help load the Bags onto the Eastern Airlines flight to Miami (there being no direct flight between the UK and Guatemala) for onward transmission on the BA flight to London. The three of us packed the Bags into the transit van, squeezed in ourselves, and off we set.

Normally, our official car was allowed to go up to the aircraft steps as the planes were always parked out on the tarmac, but not this time. The military were waiting for us, ordered us out of the van, and made us carry, or drag, the Bags, in the searing midday heat, the two hundred yards or so to the steps, to the accompaniment of jeers and derisory comments. I can't tell you how humiliating this was, and these memories too have stayed with me all these years, just like the car park ones.

Although I was still fairly weak from being ill in hospital, like Jim and Gordon, I struggled on as best I could. When we eventually reached the steps, we then had to haul the Bags up into the cabin ourselves to yet more insults. By this time the flight was very much delayed, but the Captain was very kind and understanding, appreciating what we were going through. Once inside the cabin, a soldier told us to put all the Bags on one side, but the Captain said he couldn't fly the plane with the weight so unevenly distributed, so we had to stow it all again until he was satisfied it was safe to take off. The passengers, mainly American, had tried to help us, but were ordered to remain in their seats.

Eventually the flight was set to leave. I clung to Jim, wishing so much that I could go with him. He gave me a big hug and kiss, wished Gordon and I well, and we went back onto the tarmac and watched as his plane disappeared from view. We made our way to our waiting van to yet more haranguing, but by this time neither of us cared.

Once back at the Consulate, Michael again was furious. Jim, too, was appalled at our treatment and lodged a formal complaint when he got back to London.

I met Jim a few more times after that when he came out to the Embassies in which I was working. We talked over old times: it did me good to off-load some of awful memories I still had. When I was back in London, and he was there too, he would take me out for a pub lunch, which I much enjoyed. Sadly he died a few years ago, but I can never thank him enough for all that he did for Gordon and me that day. His strength and calmness got us through that ordeal, and I will always think of him as my 'Silver Greyhound in Shining Amour'. Thank you, Jim. I'll never forget you.

The Final Humiliation

By lunchtime on Friday 12 September 1981, we were ready to leave. We had packed up as best we could: the Swiss would have to do the rest. With very heavy hearts, we closed the door for the last time on an empty Consulate-General.

The Office had managed to get us seats together on the late evening Eastern Airlines flight to Miami. It was decided that we would leave in convoy from the Residence with our heads held high. We weren't about to slink away. We loaded all our cases into the transit van, squashed into the cars we still had, and drove at breakneck speed to the airport, hotly pursued by the press and television cameras as our departure was big news. When we arrived, the military were waiting for us in full force, joined this time by a large crowd, not all well-wishers! We were very concerned for the children, but they and the wives were ushered straight into the Departure Lounge whilst we UK based were told to wait outside. There, we were ordered to open our suitcases and, in full view of everyone, tip all our personal belongings into one big pile. The Guatemalan officials then took great delight in rummaging through them, holding up certain items, and scattering them everywhere. We were then ordered to repack our cases, which meant we just had to grab whatever was to hand, whether it was ours or not, and stuff it in as best we could. At least we were allowed to take the cases to the check-in desk for them to be sent off for loading, so we didn't have to carry them ourselves. I for one was grateful for small mercies.

By this time the flight was, again, seriously delayed, but after the Diplomatic Bag fiasco I'm sure Eastern Airlines would have been aware that there was likely to be trouble, so they waited for us.

When we eventually climbed on board, I don't think any of us were prepared for the reception we received. The wives were so relieved to see us, the children were settled, but it was the reaction of our fellow passengers that was so unexpected. I think they were nearly all American – if there had been any Guatemalans, they wisely kept a low profile. We were cheered, hugged, clapped on the back, people queued to shake our hands. And all this from total strangers. We all, without exception, had tears streaming down our cheeks. I know I did. The stresses and strains of the last few days had been so hard to bear, but at last it was all over.

Once we were airborne, the Captain came into the cabin to see how we were getting on. We thanked him profusely for his understanding, and he said he was just so pleased that we were all safe. Champagne corks popped, nibbles were handed round, and we settled into our seats. For the rest of the journey, apart from the odd friendly remark as passengers passed us by to go to the loo, our privacy was respected as we came to terms with what had happened.

I had a window seat. Normally on a flight I spend a lot of time looking out the window, but this didn't happen as we flew over Guatemala. I never wanted to see that country again.

A Brief Respite

The Office, of course, had been keeping well abreast of what was happening. They were acutely aware of the state we were all in, so it had been decided that we could stay, at HMG's expense, for three nights in a very good hotel on the beach in Miami before boarding the early hours BA flight back to London. I know I was so grateful for this breathing space, as were my colleagues. I can't remember the name of the hotel. Michael and Mary were booked nearby in the first class Fontainebleau Hotel to give them peace and quiet away from everything. They did come to see us once to collect their things, but apart from that they stayed on their own, which we quite understood.

The first thing we had to do was sort out our belongings. As we were in rooms next door to each other, we put what we had stuffed into our cases in neat piles and went from room to room trying to find our own things. No point in being bashful: by the time we had finished, we knew exactly what each other had! With all this sorted out, we were then able to relax at last.

I think most of us slept for much of the time or lazed by the pool. I did. The families stayed together: Gordon, Jo and I met up in the evenings for a drink. Cars came to collect us around 2 am on the fourth day to take us to the airport, and home. When we arrived at Heathrow, I said my goodbyes to the wives and children, and went with my colleagues in official cars back to The Office for a de-briefing. I was on UK soil at last.

Miss Lofting was there waiting for me with words of comfort and support. She was concerned to see me looking so ill. We had a long talk about what had happened, but there were more pressing things that needed our immediate attention. An appointment was made for me at the Hospital for Tropical Diseases to find out what had made me so sick; and as I had nowhere to live, it was arranged for me to rent a room at the Civil Service hostel in Castle Lane, near to Birdcage Walk, until my next posting, which was already being considered.

She then said I could take a week's leave, for which I was very grateful, so I headed up to Mum and Dad in Shropshire, desperately in need of their safe and loving care. As you can imagine, it was a very emotional reunion.

Would I return to Guatemala? I don't know. It is a beautiful country and I have so much unfinished business there. *Tikal* beckons. It is, after all, one of the largest archeological sites of the pre-Columbian Maya civilization, with its more than three thousand structures. How could I not want to go there? And then there's Chichicastenango. I have unfinished shopping there too!

Were I younger, perhaps I would go back. But I'd need to lay a lot of ghosts to rest first.

Chapter Thirteen

The Falklands Conflict

My Arrival

After my traumatic time in Guatemala, I was thrilled when POD told me that my home for the next two and a half years was to be in Chile. I had longed to go there, and whilst the security situation was by no means ideal, and it was still within the Ring of Fire so prone to earthquakes yet again, I couldn't wait to go.

When I arrived in February 1982, the country was (again!) in the grip of martial law under the Pinochet regime. I'd read all I could about Chile and General Pinochet before I left London, so had a reasonable idea of what to expect. Since I had weathered the storm in Guatemala, the situation in Chile wouldn't be half as bad, I prayed.

It was what was termed a medium sized Embassy in Santiago. There were about twenty UK based staff and it was a very happy environment to work in. My Ambassador was John Moore Heath, a quiet, unassuming, kind man, whose wife Patricia I also liked. However, I would not be working for him for long as he was to retire in April, to be replaced by John Hickman.

Initially I stayed at the Hotel Orly opposite the Embassy and spent any spare time I had during my first three weeks trying to find somewhere to live. I eventually settled on a very comfortable two bed flat in a stylish block in the residential area of Providencia, not far from the Embassy. Things were looking good. I moved in a week later, and started to unpack my baggage, though most of it had sadly got 'lost' in transit between Guatemala and Chile. No surprises there, and despite representations to the Swiss, it was never found. I much looked forward to the arrival of my new white Escort (paid for with another FCO Car Loan) which was being shipped out and was due to arrive sometime mid-March.

All was going swimmingly when there was a dramatic turn of events.

The Falklands Conflict
(Not a war, as war was never officially declared)

On 2 April 1982 the Argentinians invaded the Falkland Islands, in the southern Atlantic, and once again I was 'embroiled' in a territorial dispute. Cue Victor Meldrew. *I DON'T BELIEVE IT!* I was beginning to think I should pay him royalties! When could I stop uttering these words, I asked myself? Shades of my traumatic time in Guatemala all over again. Would I ever have a peaceful posting?

A Brief Background
There always seem to be disputes between Spain and its former colonies and Great Britain. Spain and Gibraltar first spring to mind, and this still rumbles on. In Guatemala it was over Belize.

In Argentina, it was the Falkland Islands (or the Islas Malvinas as the Argentinians call them) and the two South Atlantic British dependent territories, South Georgia and the South Sandwich Islands. Argentina has always claimed that it had inherited these islands from Spain before they were occupied by the British in 1833 and became a Crown colony in 1841.

Thus, the conflict in 1982 was regarded by Argentina as a legitimate reclamation of its own territory. On 2 April (I remember that day vividly), Argentina invaded and occupied the Falkland Islands, followed the next day by the invasion of South Georgia. On 5 April the British Government dispatched a naval task force to fight against the Argentine Air Force and Navy before making an amphibious assault on the islands.

The conflict lasted seventy-two days (it seemed like an eternity to us) and ended with Argentina surrendering on 14 June. The Islands were then returned to British control. Six hundred and forty-nine Argentinian soldiers, two hundred and fifty-five British military personnel, and three Falkland Islanders lost their lives during these hostilities.

Full diplomatic relations between the UK and Argentina were restored in 1989 after a meeting of the two governments in Madrid and the issuing of a joint statement. However, there was no change in either government's position on the sovereignty of the Falkland Islands, and in 1994 Argentina adopted a new constitution which declared that the Islands were one of its provinces by law. And so this dispute rumbles on too! But the Islands continue to be a self-governing British Overseas Territory, much to the relief of the islanders, who are mainly descendants of British settlers from the 19th century and wish to remain British.

It has now been openly acknowledged that Chile played an important role in helping the British defeat the Argentinians in this Conflict. It was felt that a successful Argentine campaign in the Falklands would then encourage Argentina to attack Chile. Margaret Thatcher made reference to it when she expressed support for General Pinochet whilst he was in custody in the UK from 1998 to 2000 on a Spanish warrant on human rights charges.

Later, after the publication of *The Official History of the Falklands War* in June 2007, Tony Blair sent a copy of the chapter on Chile to the Chilean President, Ricardo Lagos, who, according to the Argentine Ambassador, shared it with his Argentine counterpart, Nestor Kirchner.

Life in the Embassy during the Falklands Conflict

Britain broke off diplomatic relations with Argentina on 2 April and the majority of the UK Embassy staff in Buenos Aires went to Montevideo. After my own traumatic time in Guatemala, how I sympathized with them! But whilst they were having a torrid time, we in the Embassy in Santiago were also very much involved in the Conflict. Overnight our lives changed. The locally employed continued working more or less normally, but we UK-based were put on shift work, and of necessity what we were doing was kept strictly secret from our Chilean employees on the floors below our Chancery.

We were in our own fortress, with comings and goings happening mostly in the middle of the night, despite the curfew. The soldiers manning the checkpoints, on seeing our Diplomatic number plates, waved us through with no questions asked. I well remember also on one occasion having to drive round Santiago on a Sunday trying to find our Defence Attaché (DA). I even had to stop the morning service at St Andrew's to ask if he was there. I did eventually find him, thank goodness, but he was not where I had thought he would be! Bearing in mind I had only arrived in Santiago in February, and had had my car a fortnight, getting to know my way around the city was proving to be a steep learning curve!

Because of the Conflict also, our UK 'workforce' multiplied overnight, particularly in the Defence Section. Our resident DA was a Naval Captain, it being the Navy's turn to be represented, but it immediately became clear that an Air Attaché was urgently needed as well to bolster up that Section and liaise with the Chilean Air Force over the use of their airbases etc. Wing Commander Sidney Edwards was sent out, and he proved indispensable. He was a great character, calm, very funny, and he did his best (and succeeded) in keeping up morale when we were beginning to flag through the stresses and strains of it all. Thank you, Sid. You really made a difference.

Sid established an immediate rapport with General Fernando Matthei, the head of the Chilean Air Force, and I know there was a great mutual respect on both sides.

(You can read all about his involvement in his book 'My Secret Falklands War' published in July 2014 under the thirty-year rule.)

Once the Conflict ended, our Naval DA returned home as it was the end of his tour, and he was replaced by Squadron Leader Brian Batt (later Air Commodore) as resident DA since it was then the turn of the Air Force. Brian was equally good fun, and we had some laughs. Sid stayed on for a little while after, but then returned to the UK to take up another position.

Being Ambassador's PA meant that I had a very high security clearance. On the work front, I spent many a happy (?) hour glued to our **Noreen** cypher machine, knee deep in Murray Code tape. As I said before, operating it was slow and laborious, and required great concentration. It was also so tiring, and my eyes ached. I began to see permanent dots before them! Any typo meant the dots were wrong and you had to read them back and sort it out. And woe betide anyone who came near the tape and broke it.

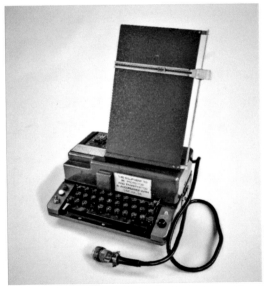

Just a reminder! Because I loved you so much, **NOREEN**!
©Crown Copyright, by kind permission Director, GCHQ

I well remember one occasion, when the battery and spare were both low, asking Celia, our Chancery PA, to go and fill them with distilled water. She immediately got a jug and filled them with tap water instead, which meant they wouldn't work. I then spent the morning driving round Santiago visiting all the garages I could find, trying to obtain suitable replacements. How I loved her! By now I was getting to be an expert in areas of the city I wouldn't have dreamt of visiting, and all this with only a street guide. No Satnav in those days! But it worked wonders for my everyday Spanish. Then, miracle of miracles, a much-needed new modern machine, *Alvis,* arrived and was duly installed, which made our lives a lot easier. But there must have been over seventeen hundred groups of dots on the tape that we never did manage to decipher before *Alvis*. I wonder what they said?

STUFT

On a personal front, I was dismayed that my beloved P&O ships **ss CANBERRA and ss UGANDA** were involved in the Conflict too. I worried about them a lot. Both ships came under the heading of STUFT (Ships Taken Up from Trade, that is a civilian ship requisitioned for government use). **CANBERRA** was requisitioned off Gibraltar on 4 May.

Both ships were very dear to my heart. The initial plan, once **CANBERRA** arrived in the Falklands, was to use her as a floating field hospital, but being so large, she was a prime target for air strikes despite her protected status and would need to be kept two hundred miles out to sea, which was impractical. She was then used for landing and embarking troops, as well as offloading supplies and military equipment. This meant she was now without doubt a prime target, lying so conspicuous and exposed at anchor in San Carlos Sound. I kept abreast of all that was happening through the mountain of messages I was decoding, and at one point managed to exchange a brief message with the love of my life who was a very senior officer on board. We needed to check that the other was safe. and coping, as we were. But he said being in **CANBERRA** was so tough, and quite terrifying at times. How I wish I could have been in Southampton to see **CANBERRA's** homecoming after serving her country so valiantly. I watched on Chilean television, with many tears and a very thankful heart.

P&O's ss CANBERRA in San Carlos Sound.
I could weep when I see her like this.
(© P&O Heritage – www.poheritage.com)

P&O's ss UGANDA as a hospital ship during the Falklands Conflict
(© P&O Heritage – www.poheritage.com)

UGANDA, being a hospital ship, was protected under The Geneva Convention (GWS-Sea). She had to be respected at all times and under no circumstances was to be attacked or captured. She was under the command of Surgeon Captain Rick Jolly, who was the only Serviceman to be honoured by both the British and Argentinian sides for managing three frontline field hospitals in which over one thousand casualties, including three hundred Argentinian soldiers and airmen, were successfully treated. Of great pride to those on board.

Keep Calm, and Carry On

Whilst all this was happening, I was trying outwardly to maintain as normal a working routine and appearance as possible. Not easy, but I managed, and the Ambassador, bless him, was calmness personified, which made all the difference to the atmosphere in the Embassy. Social contacts still had to be cultivated, dinners and receptions held, though there were much fewer of them. Fortunately, Elspeth, the locally employed Social Secretary, who normally dealt with Residence staff and Patricia's social diary, was able to help with these entertaining matters, leaving me free for the extra duties I had to do. She was invaluable and I was so grateful.

I worked on steadily. Report after report, telegram after telegram. They just wouldn't stop coming, but it was so very interesting, despite the seriousness and tragedy of it all.

Operation *Mikardo* (now in the public domain)

This was the code name of a military plan to use our SAS troops to attack the Argentine airbase at Rio Grandé in Tierra del Fuego, from where Argentina's five Super Étendard fighter aircraft, firing Exocet missiles, had made their successful sorties against our troops and had sunk two ships. Brigadier Peter de la Billière was in charge of this operation. The plan was also for our men to kill the pilots of these aircraft in their quarters.

Each of our SAS soldiers was fluent in Latin American Spanish, as distinct from Castilian Spanish, which resurrected memories of colonialism. (I learned very early on when I arrived in Peru that I had to lose my Castilian accent in order to survive in Latin America!) The soldiers were also South American in appearance and would have blended in well.

To achieve the operation's objective, the Brigadier also planned a tandem operation whereby fifty-five SAS soldiers and two Lockheed C-130s Hercules aircraft would land directly on the runway at Rio Grande to destroy the Super Étendards. The C-130s would be kept running whilst the SAS men carried out their mission. If the C-130s survived, they would head for the Chilean air base at Punta Arenas. If not, any surviving members of the SAS Squadron would make their way as best they could to the Chilean border, about fifty miles to the west, and then on to us.

Even I was about to play a minor role in all this. Despite being the Ambassador's PA, it was hoped that, as a single female, it would never occur to any informants/spies that I would be involved in the Conflict at a practical level. Thus, on two separate occasions I smuggled an SAS soldier out of the Embassy in the boot of my car in the middle of the night and hid him in my flat for two days so that he could recover after his fraught journey up from the south.

We never talked about work, though I did share one or two funny experiences, like the saga of the batteries, which they found highly amusing. Typical woman was the general consensus. Not wishing to enter into a battle of the sexes, I agreed wholeheartedly. Anyway, I hadn't been the one to do it, fortunately.

These two men (I knew them only by the Chilean names they had been given), were not in good shape. They were exhausted, disheveled, very hungry, and obviously affected by what they had been through. All they wanted to do was have a hot shower, and just sleep. I prepared substantial meals for them, for which they were

Argentine Navy Dassault-Breguet Super Étendard fighter as used in
Operation Mikardo, in 1982.
(Photograph used under Creative Commons License Deed (CC BY 2.5)

very grateful. Even though I'm not the world's best cook, I'm sure my
food tasted better than nothing!

At this time Chancery looked like a charity shop. We had collected
all sorts of second-hand, 'working class' civilian clothing from
wherever we could, arranged it in sizes and used it when needed. I
collected what I thought 'my' two men would need: trousers, shirts,
jackets, socks and shoes (underpants were a bit tricky) and hoped
they would more or less fit, which they did, though we did have a
laugh at the end result. They would never have won a 'best dressed
man' award, but they were inconspicuous and blended in well with
the local population, which was after all the object of the exercise.

When it was time for them to go, I smuggled them out of the flat in
the boot in the dead of night and took them back to the Embassy for
onward transport to who knows where. I never knew what happened
to them after that, but I have the utmost admiration for their bravery
and what they did.

In the end **Operation *Mikardo*** was abandoned. It was already being considered a suicide mission by experienced SAS soldiers, which caused great hostility towards it. It was impossible pull off because of the loss of the element of surprise due to British intelligence having under-estimated the capability of the Argentinian radar system. We didn't have a clear idea of how the base was defended, nor organized, nor whether in fact the planes and missiles would be there when we thought they would be. It was therefore deemed too risky to proceed and the Operation was ended.

On a lighter note, I still have a cartoon (too faded to reproduce I'm afraid) of an Exocet missile, an 'Exo-boomerang', going round in a circle and smashing straight into the *Casa Rosada* (the President's Palace) in Buenos Aires. It was displayed in a prominent part of Chancery, to the great enjoyment of us all!

What it is to be loved!

We couldn't believe the length of the queues outside the Embassy, of Chileans of all ages keen to join up. Chile and Argentina were on the brink of war four years earlier because of a dispute (yet another one!) over three islands in the Beagle Channel, and it was only a last-minute intervention by Pope John Paul II that avoided this. So there was definitely no love lost between the two countries.

All this time, it was also like living with a pop star! Sacks of 'fan mail' kept arriving, driving our Admin Section mad. Most of the letters contained small amounts of money, notes and coins, from well-wishers eager to help towards our costs! It was all so very touching.

The End of the Conflict

On 14 June, after seventy-two agonizing days, the Argentinians surrendered. I cannot tell you the feelings of relief, tinged with great sadness at the needless loss of life, when it was announced.

Not that that is the end of it, unfortunately. As I said, Argentina still views the Falkland Islands as part of its territory, but thanks to their self-government, and the amount of inward investment and sale of fishing licences etc, they are now quite prosperous. Today they are defended by twelve hundred British military troops at an annual cost to the UK of about £60 million.

My Own Thoughts
On a personal front, I have been immensely proud to have played my part, however small that might have been, in ensuring the Islands remain British. Wars and conflicts always hide dirty secrets. The loss of life was tragic on both sides No-one can dispute that, and to those who gave their lives, we as a nation and the Falkland Islanders in particular, owe a huge debt of gratitude.

Last year (2022) was the 40th anniversary (is it really that long ago?) since the Conflict took place. There have been many acts of remembrance, the most poignant for me being the Remembrance Service at the Royal Albert Hall. I cannot help but be immensely moved and emotional when I think back to all that happened in those seventy-two days, and so very grateful that it has been, and will be, remembered and acknowledged so publicly.

Picking Up the Pieces
With the end of the Conflict, at last I could hopefully get back to some sort of normality. My life (as with us all) had been put on hold for seventy-two days. Now it was time to get out and about, make friends, join clubs, play golf, go to parties. Start living once again in my new surroundings.

But first things first. I was anxious to finish unpacking as there were still one or two big boxes I hadn't had time to sort out and items in them that I needed. There were also pictures and small pieces of furniture I wanted to buy for the flat to make it more homely and to my taste. Retail therapy works wonders, especially after such a harrowing time.

One task I could tick off, though, was 'orientation'. One of the first things I always do when arriving at a new post is to take the streetmap and just drive around in my spare time, getting lost, finding my way back, and any 'back doubles' I can take. However, after all my various local sorties during the Conflict, I felt I was now qualified to give any Chilean taxi driver a good run for his money!

14 June 1982 – After the Argentine surrender.
The British flag flies once more in the Falkland Islands outside the
Residence in Port Stanley of the Governor, Sir Rex Hunt.
A jubilant moment. (Credit: John W. Jockel)

On the work front, the Ambassador started to pack up as he could now look forward to his retirement at last, and I got ready for my new boss, John Hickman. I was busier than ever arranging all the farewell receptions and dinners for John and Patricia as they were a very popular couple. I knew I'd miss him (them) as he had been brilliant to work for, but I was so happy they were returning to Bath to a more settled life.

A Very Unexpected Invitation
As a post-script to this Chapter on the Falklands, when I was posted to Budapest from 1991-1994, our Minister and Chargé in the Ambassador's absence was Howard Pearce. His PA, Carol, who became a good friend, and I shared an office, with Howard's office on Carol's side and the Ambassador's on mine. The four of us had

many a laugh together, though Carol and I worked exceedingly hard, particularly during The State Visit.

I liked Howard a lot. He was four years younger than me, and we were both single. I had the distinct feeling (so did Carol) that my Ambassador would have been happy if we had become 'an item'. When I asked him directly a few years ago, he gave a very non-committal answer, but there was a mischievous glint in his eye, which made me think I was right. I was regularly partnered with Howard at dinner parties and receptions, and quite often acted as his hostess when he returned the hospitality. I even went to stay with him for two days at his home in Oxfordshire, but we were just really good friends and never destined to be 'that item'! Sorry John!

After leaving Budapest I then went back to London on a home posting. Howard and I kept in touch until he was posted as Governor to the Falkland Islands from December 2002 to July 2006.

I was working at the time for the Director (Under-Secretary of State) for Wider Europe when a very smart envelope turned up in my mail tray one day in September 2004. I opened it and couldn't believe my eyes. It was a Wedding Invitation to Howard's marriage to Caroline Thomée, a Dutch architect and photographer (whom I don't know). I was thrilled for him: it was so kind of him to remember me. But I was even more excited when I saw where the wedding venue was: Port Stanley in the Falkland Islands (how I wish I had that venue now I'm a Registrar of Marriages, but it's a bit out of our area here in West Sussex).

I was desperate to accept the invitation. It would be great to catch up with Howard again, and for me the prospect of going to the Falklands and seeing all the places I had known about during the Conflict was an added draw, I must admit.

I started to plan, but then sadly reality set in when I saw what it would cost. At that time, church mouse and I were on very neighborly terms as I had spent nearly all my savings on the deposit for a flat. I would have to pay my own expenses, of course, and the cost of a return flight on a military aircraft from Brize Norton to Port Stanley was almost £1000. Then there was the cost of a hotel for four days, plus a wedding present. Credit cards were not so widely used then (at least I didn't have one), so I couldn't put the cost on that. I added it all up, and with great sadness and reluctance I decided that I just couldn't afford it and therefore had to regret. I can't tell you how disappointed I was.

Howard was disappointed, too, that I couldn't attend, he said, and to this day I really wish I could have gone. If you ever read this, Howard: thank you so much for the thought, and I hope you are both very happy.

Chapter Fourteen

Peacekeeping

I went 'yomping' with the Army across Salisbury Plain! 'Yomping' is the Royal Marines slang, popularized during the Falklands Conflict, for going on a long march carrying full gear. It must have been awful trudging over that hostile terrain, under such a weight, but I had cause myself, in a very small way, to appreciate what they had gone through.

I was back in London after Hungary, on the last 'leg' of my career with The Office. I was working for the Director Wider Europe, John Macgregor at the time, and one of the Departments for which he was responsible was OSCE (Organisation for Security and Co-operation in Europe – the world's largest regional security organization). The main problem occupying this Department when I was there was the aftermath of the Bosnian [Civil] War (1991-1995) which had started as a result of the fall of communism, when Bosnia and Herzegovina joined several republics of the former Yugoslavia which had declared their independence. This conflict had ended with United Nations sanctions and UN air strikes, which finally brought the warring parties to the negotiating table and peace was restored.

However, trying to maintain this peace was another matter, and it was the OSCE's role to do so, part of which required a military presence in the region. At this time Paddy Ashdown [later Baron Ashdown of Norton-sub-Hamdon] had been appointed as High Representative for Bosnia and Herzegovina (2002-2006) and was a frequent visitor to John's office. I liked him a lot, and he always had time for a brief chat.

To further the knowledge of the staff of OSCE Department on this subject, it was arranged for them to go on a twenty-four hour 'away-day' training exercise with the Army on Salisbury Plain. John and I were to go too, which for me was a wonderful opportunity to learn more about the situation in the region and what was involved in keeping things on an even keel.

I thought nothing of the request to bring warm clothing and heavy walking boots. After all, we would be outside a bit, familiarising ourselves with the Army Camp at Tidworth, where we would be based, plus attending the odd lecture or so in between. Nothing to worry about there. So, after lunch on a day in November 2003 (I forget the exact date), twelve of us, and rucksacks, set off in a minibus heading for the Camp

On arrival, we were introduced to the CO and the Army officers who would be looking after us and given a welcome cup of tea.

The first thing we had to do was fill in a health questionnaire. Strange, I thought, for a stroll around the Camp and a lecture or two. It must be an Army regulation. So, I filled in the form, handed it back to a soldier, and thought no more about it.

Then our briefing began. I would be billeted (sharing a room) with the Head of Department's PA. Fine. However, when we were sent off to be kitted out with 'fatigues', a large torch, and a backpack which would contain dried rations and our warm clothes, reality set in. No sauntering around the Camp for us. Worse still, we were told we would be woken up at 0300 to begin the training exercise on the Plain. This was not in my plan, but not to worry, I consoled myself. All part of the excitement of the outing. After that, I retired to bed to snatch an hour or two of sleep but lay awake most of the time.

At 0300 there was a loud banging on our door; we were given a small ration for breakfast, and then driven somewhere onto Salisbury Plain. There we were offloaded from the Army transport vehicle and abandoned in the middle of nowhere in the dead of night. Of course, we had Army personnel with us, but it was scary - pitch black causing us to stumble over the uneven ground. And an accident occurred when the young secretary badly twisted her ankle by stepping down a rabbit hole! Not a good start. She was taken back to Tidworth by one of our accompanying soldiers, where she had to stay all day until we returned.

We were split into groups of three and our first task was to scour the area, in the dark, and find an old barn, which eventually we managed to locate. There we had to search for explosives and ammunition (not live, of course – at least I hoped not) amongst all the hay and farming machinery. This I did with great gusto, more to keep warm than anything else as it was freezing cold. And I did indeed find some sticks of dynamite on a platform at one end of the barn. Our soldiers were very impressed as they were well hidden, and I hoped these Brownie points would stand me in good stead for what was to follow (whatever that was). No chance!

Training with the Army on Salisbury Plain
John Macgregor (with hat), Peter January, Head of OSCE Department,
and me (and one of our 'helpers').

After that, a welcome cup of coffee, more dried rations (not scintillating), and off again trudging over the countryside to our next destination, a large tent (in the photo) where we were instructed on the Army's counter-terrorism activities in Bosnia: how to spot troublemakers; how to secure buildings; how to identify forged documents; how to process people from different ethnic communities and religions; how to instill confidence within the local community, and Human Rights guidelines. I found all this absolutely fascinating. I learned so much and could have stayed there all day (in the comparative warmth).

But it was not to be, of course. Time for lunch. More rations (ah well, at least I should lose a bit of weight today) and then, joy of joys, the noise of a helicopter landing nearby. I love them. This was more like it. And I was even more excited when told I was going up in it. Brilliant. This was worth all the pain and starvation. I was in the first group to go up and it was super. I loved every minute of it, swooping down over Salisbury Plain like a hawk homing in on its prey. Some of my colleagues looked a bit green around the gills, but I thrived on it. I love flying (just as well in my job) and this was the icing on the cake.

But sadly, we couldn't ride around in the helicopter all day. Back on the ground, for our last task. We set off at intervals to march about a mile uphill to a thicket, still carrying our backpacks which by now felt like a ton weight (well mine did anyway). There we had to find a rifle, sling it over our shoulder and march two miles back to the Camp, by this time in the semi-dark.

For someone who, aged 57 and who liked to spend most of her spare time on the golf course or a tennis court, with a weekly Tai Chi session thrown in to 'energise the spirit', I thought I was fairly fit, but this was proving a bit of a challenge to say the least. Eventually I found a rifle (don't know what sort) in some brambles, hoisted it over my sagging shoulder, and ploughed on, taking heart as I saw John and my colleagues struggling just as much as me. At last – finally - I reached the Camp where there was cake (goodness me) and a cup of tea. About time too, I thought.

After that, our thanks and farewells to the CO and our soldiers, who had been very patient with us, though they had stood no nonsense. They must have thought we were a complete load of wimps, but we had all done our best.

We collapsed into the minibus and headed back to London. By the time we got back it was dark, and I don't know how I had the strength to get out of the bus, let alone walk to Victoria Station to catch my train home. I ached all over and was famished. But in true PA spirit, I had gritted my teeth, overcome adversity and succeeded! Whew. Well done, that girl!

On reflection, it had been a most memorable and instructive outing. Well worth all the pulled muscles. Personally, I had benefited so much from spending this time with the Army. I now understood far better the situation in Bosnia and Herzegovina, the problems the OSCE forces faced on a daily basis, and it certainly made my job that much more interesting and seemingly worthwhile as a result. And Paddy Ashdown was delighted to hear what we had done too.

After twenty years, I have never forgotten that 'away-day'.

Getting to grips with it all.   A dream come true!

PART SEVEN

My Leisure and Sport Abroad

Chapter Fifteen

My Leisure Time

My Leisure Time

In all the Embassies in which I have worked, we strove to be one big happy family. Occasionally there was frustration caused by the environment in which we were living, and we had a good moan, but we made a conscious effort to get on, which we did. We spent a lot of time in each other's company outside of the Embassy and organized some great parties and outings between us. We usually got together at Christmas for a traditional Christmas lunch, whether with the Ambassador, H of C or another Head of Section, and birthdays were always celebrated.

The most special birthday treats for me were the trips to the floating market and islands (*chinampas*) at *Xochimilco* in Mexico, where a group of us would hire a boat, along with a band of excellent *mariachis,* loaded it up with beer and food, and set off down the canals with dozens of other boats all with the same idea. The noise of the different musicians all playing different tunes at different times was so deafening it was difficult to pick out a tune, but we sang along anyway, no matter. And it was a big challenge for our 'skipper' to navigate his way around all the other crafts. But the atmosphere was unbelievable, and we never failed to have such a fantastic time. It set us up well for the week ahead. Other Embassy outings included a steep climb up Taal Volcano outside of Manila; weekends away fishing and also skiing in Austria; evenings at the races at the *Club Hípico* in Santiago – to name but a few.

And of course, if my leave didn't coincide with that of any of my colleagues, I went off either on my own, or with a friend from another Embassy or an ex-pat. Usually, we stayed fairly near to the capital, but in Peru my best friend Barbara (the New Zealand Ambassador's PA) and I drove to Ica and hired a Cessna to fly over the ancient Inca

On my 45th birthday at *Xochimilco*

Nazca Lines. It was a novel experience, though I omitted to tell Barbara, who was sitting in the back of the plane, that there were quite a few gauges missing in the aircraft. She would have had a fit.

I was heartbroken when, two months later, Barbara had to be medi-vacced back to New Zealand and died a few days later from liver cancer. She hadn't been too well at Ica, but neither of us had anticipated this. I signed the Book of Condolence at the New Zealand Embassy. I did miss her - a lot.

My Own Visitors
Because I was always posted so far away, dear Mum and Dad could never afford to visit me. I missed them dreadfully and relied so much on their weekly letters. I wrote copious letters back – which I found in a shoe box in the attic after Mum had died. We also managed the odd phone call on birthdays and Christmas, but it wasn't the same. One of the redeeming features about being posted to Hungary, though, was that at last they could come out to stay, which they did for twelve days in September 1992. I couldn't spend all that time with them because of work, but the Ambassador very kindly gave me the odd half day off, and also invited them to lunch

Mum and Dad at Szentendre

at the Residence, which they much enjoyed, though Dad, being shy, was petrified at the thought at first.

Each evening we looked at the map to see where they would like to go that wasn't too far away. I gave them all the information, dropped them off on my way to work near to where they were going that day, and they found their way back to the Embassy for me to take them home. I was amazed. Neither of them spoke any foreign languages, but they seemed quite happy just wandering around on their own. We didn't realize at the time that Dad was beginning to suffer from Parkinsons, but they managed well. I was so pleased. Then at the weekend we took off each day and travelled further afield to Esztergom, the Danube Bend, Visegrad and Lake Balaton, all of which they loved.

I was so sad to see them go but I knew that they were within easy reach at last.

Pam's Visits

Then came my dear friend, Pam. We left P&O at about the same time, and Pam went to work for British Caledonian, later British Airways, as part of the check-in staff whilst I joined The Office. This was ideal as she then had access to concession flights, and so she became my most regular visitor.

We had some wonderful outings together. In the Philippines it was to Baguio, then by local bus, with squealing pigs slung underneath it, through the mountains to Sagada, staying on the way back to Manila at the Thousand Islands beach resort for two days.

Pam visited me twice in Chile, and again we had two memorable excursions.

The AURA *Observatorio Interamericano* at Cerro Tololo

The first one was a visit, arranged by the Ambassador, to the AURA *Observatorio Interamericano* at Cerro Tololo, high up in the Andes, where we were shown around by one of the astronomers. So very interesting. The view was amazing, but then this location was especially chosen for the clarity of the atmosphere, making planetary observations excellent.

Our journey back down the mountain was equally memorable, but in a different way. We got caught in an earthquake when we were in a remote village buying rations. Tins were flying off the shelves all around us, and we knew it was imperative that we got to the foot of this mountain as quickly as possible. I drove like the clappers, hardly able to see where I was going for the dust swirling around us. Scree and rocks were sliding down onto the road, and we only just made it back down to sea level. We were both shaking when we reached the bottom: a terrifying experience, but at least we were safe.

Then on her next visit we put the car on the train down to Puerto Montt, and flew on to Punta Arenas, visiting the *Torres del Paine* National Park, which was spectacular, even though unfortunately the *Torres* (mountain peaks) were shrouded in mist.

Pam and me at the *Torres del Paine* National Park

In Mexico, on her first visit we drove to Taxco (good for buying silver) and on to Acapulco for a relaxing two days. On her next stay, we went west to Pátzcuaro via Morelia (now unfortunately drug baron country), and also spent time at the Pyramids of Teotihuacán.

And in Hungary Pam came out this time with our other P&O friend, Tricia, and we spent most of the time in and around Budapest.

Had it not been for Pam, I wouldn't have seen half of what I did see, and we often still relive our experiences of these trips. Thanks, Pam.

Other good friends came and went: my New Zealand neighbour, Lorna, from Manila; Erwan (EU Ambassador to Mexico). I was so pleased not only to see them again, but also to offer them hospitality. We have all survived, and I am still in touch with them. We often look back, as I do with Pam, on our very happy times together in foreign parts.

Looking at the Stars!

Mexico turned out to be the country where I really rubbed shoulders with celebrities.

I was very friendly with Harry Clements, the single Head of Unilever in Mexico, and often attended his functions and partnered him when needed. He was my age, but there was no romantic attachment. We were just really good friends.

Harry rang me one evening to ask if I would like to accompany him to a Charity Concert, in *Nauhatl* (the Aztec language), being given by Plácido Domingo at the Pyramids of Teotihuacán. This was the first time a concert had been performed in this language and it was considered a very important occasion. I was absolutely thrilled to be asked, and of course accepted with great excitement. The dress code was full evening dress. Being at night at altitude meant it would be very cold, so I borrowed a fur coat from an ex-pat friend of mine, though my feet fared less better even with the cashmere blanket Harry had brought for both of us. Being a Charity event, and given his position within the commercial community, Harry had paid $US300 each for our tickets, no small amount in 1988, but it did ensure that we had front row seats and were two of the few invited to the dinner with the maestro afterwards.

It was fabulous. I didn't understand a word, but that didn't matter. And at the dinner afterwards, held in the gardens of a nearby Convent, I chatted with Maestro Domingo when he joined our table. We wined and dined, with the dessert finally being served at around 4 am. I needed to be home by 10 am though, as our Admin Officer, Alan, was due to collect me to take me to the American British Cowdray Hospital for my hysterectomy, which he did. The memories of that evening sustained me during that time, but there was another encounter that was even more special.

A week or so before the concert, I had been busy typing one day when the phone rang. "Good afternoon, it's Timothy Dalton here." Well, I nearly dropped the phone in astonishment. I knew he was in Mexico for the filming of 'Licence to Kill' but he needed help with a certain matter. I was able to assist, and he invited me down to Churubusco Studios to watch the filming whenever I wanted. I was down there like a shot and got to know Tim and some of the crew fairly well. Tim and I had a bartering arrangement: English tea bags (which I had) for baked beans (which he had – despite all the beans in Mexico, there weren't any baked ones!) and this worked really well. I also arranged medical appointments for anyone who needed one, and even took June (Continuity) and Jack (Makeup Artist) and his wife down to our Embassy guest house in Cuernavaca for a weekend's R&R.

Those members of the cast and crew whom I knew were aware I was going into hospital, and sent me a big bouquet of flowers, which was such a kind gesture. I then had five weeks convalescence until I had my surgeon's clearance to go back to work. In the meantime, once I was more or less mobile, a car was sent up from the Studios to take me down there to continue watching filming (part of my own important R&R, I justified). I did get a telling off from Robert Davi for inadvertently sitting in his Directors chair, but apart from that, everything went perfectly and I had the most unforgettable time, though it was hard not to burst my stitches because of some of the hilarious 'mishaps' that occurred. Trade secrets though. Sorry!

Jill Thanks & Bestwishes
Tim.

On the set of 'Licence to Kill'

When it was a 'wrap', I was even invited to buy any costume items that were going on sale (they don't do this now). I chose Della Leiter's lace wedding shoes, and a somewhat risqué but beautiful evening dress from the casino scene. I kept both items for a long time, even wearing the dress to the opera when Princess Diana came to Budapest. Eventually, though, I had no further use for them (more to the point, the dress no longer fitted), and they went to auction.

But that wasn't the end. I was back in the UK on mid-tour-leave from Mexico when I received an invitation from Iris Rose to attend the première of 'Licence to Kill' in Leicester Square. I couldn't believe it. What a thrill. I didn't have a partner to take with me, so as I was staying with Pam, I asked her if she would like to go too. Needless to say, she did. It was the most magical evening, and it gave me the chance to catch up with my film crew friends. I even got a brief hello from Tim, but he was very much in demand, as you can imagine.

I often watch that film and it brings back such happy memories. All the amusing incidents, the minor mishaps, the re-taking of scenes time after time. I can even see my dress walking by!

Wearing my James Bond somewhat risqué dress!
(With my Hungarian escort for the evening, Zoltán, at the Budapest Opera for the visit of HRH Princess Diana)

Cadfael
Budapest is also an important film-making centre, and I was fortunate enough to be invited to the Föt Studios just outside of the city to watch *Cadfael* being filmed. I love this series, especially with its Shrewsbury connection (where Mum and Dad lived). I went twice and was enthralled. I also enjoyed talking to Derek Jacobi for brief moments between shots. Filming this series wasn't without its risks for him, though, especially when he had a nasty fall off a donkey. I closed my ears on that occasion!

Grand Prix
As well as sport, I love my cars, and Grand Prix in particular, and I used to go with Dad to Silverstone and Donnington Park when we could. Once abroad, I indulged this interest in Mexico with my

On the set of *Cadfael* at the Föt Studios, Budapest

doctor boyfriend Román, also an avid enthusiast, at the *Hermanos Rodriguez* Circuit; and in Hungary, at the *Hungaroring* at Mogyoród near Budapest. My absolute favourite was Martin Brundle, who came second there. I was thrilled. I became a member of his Supporters Club, spending great Saturdays with him, when in the UK, at Silverstone when he was testing with Jordan. He was always so generous with his time, arranging lunch for us, and then thrashing us at go-karting.

The 1994 Grand Prix at the Hungaroring, Mogyoród

Nigel Mansell paid a visit to the Embassy too and was presented with a racehorse by the Hungarian Racing Authority in Vörösmarty tér, nearby. When they said horsepower, I'm not sure this is what he expected, but he accepted it graciously. Getting it back to the UK was a problem, and I don't think it ever won, but it was a kind gesture. Well, I thought so!

Gliding

To end this Chapter on a high note, so to speak, when I was in Santiago Ross, our Second Secretary, decided he would like to get his Gliding Pilot's Licence, so he applied himself diligently to the course and was successful, much to the Ambassador's pride and delight. He was then eager to take us up in his glider, and I was keen to fly with him. The Ambassador was slightly less keen for his PA to be swooping over the lower Andes but said I could go. We had some wonderful flights together on the air currents swirling around the mountains, and it seemed strange to look out of the cockpit window and be on the same level as the majestic condors who were keeping us company. The peace and quiet was a welcome respite from the hustle of the city below, and the views were spectacular.

There was one heart-stopping moment, though, when the towing cable snapped with an almighty crack and came whizzing past us at breakneck speed. We didn't know what had caused it to fail, but fortunately we had only just commenced the tow and were still on the ground at the time. Luckily, it hadn't damaged the glider either. We agreed not to tell the Ambassador about that incident.

There were, of course, many more interests and activities that I pursued when at Post, and this Chapter is only a taster of how I occupied my precious leisure time. Wherever I was, though, I tried to get the most out of it and, looking back, I think I can honestly say that I succeeded.

Chapter Sixteen

Sport Abroad

Sport has always been my passion and whilst, because of my chosen careers, it has not always been easy to indulge this passion, I have tried my best to do so as you will see.

Golf

At last, when I was posted to **Manila**, I was able to take up my tennis again at the Intercontinental Hotel, but more importantly, it was there that I learned to play golf, which I had been longing to do for many years.

I had an excellent teaching pro, Carlos, and because of my hockey, I quickly progressed under his tuition, although I did have to remember at times not to wield the club like a hockey stick. I became a member of the Fort Bonifacio Golf Club, not being able to afford the exclusive Manila or Wack Wack (yes, really) Golf Clubs, and within a short time, I had a handicap which allowed me to play in competitions with a reasonable amount of success. I followed Carlos during his tournaments, and because of him became involved in the golfing scene in general, even being on nodding terms with President Marcos, himself a golf fanatic, whom we would meet on various courses around Manila, surrounded by a host of security men of course.

I also became a helper at major events, on one occasion marking for Bob Byman, a ranked American golfer, at the World Cup at Nichols Airbase. It was at that tournament also that I met two up and coming 'youngsters', Nick Faldo and Ken Brown, at the reception held for the event. Lively lads, and very pleasant!

But golf in the Philippines was fraught with danger, I soon discovered, mainly because of venomous **snakes**. I have a great fear of them, but they seemed to be everywhere. When driving alone after a tournament in Southern Luzon, I ran over a **python** that had been lurking in the sugar canes either side of the road. I thought it was a piece of cane, and only realized what it was just before I hit it. Even though I don't like them, I would never knowingly hurt one, but on this occasion I wasn't getting out of the car to see if it was alright. But it did give me quite a scare.

As if pythons weren't bad enough, at the Filipinas Golf Club outside Manila where Carlos and I used to play regularly, it was **cobras**.

There had been a **cobra** farm where the Golf Club now was, but during the War it had been bombed and most of the inmates had escaped and had taken up residence in the bamboo and sugar cane fields bordering the course. Not ideal. And on one particular occasion, it certainly wasn't for me.

I was having a good day. I'd just shot an Eagle on the par five and had hit a cracking drive on the next par four: Carlos was impressed. Birdie here, no problem. I was sauntering along, kicking the dap-dap tree leaves that had fallen on the fairway when all of a sudden, my caddy grabbed my nine iron and started bashing the ground immediately in front of me. Funny, I thought. I didn't think I was doing that badly. He then proceeded to scoop something up off the ground, and I saw to my absolute horror a dead, bloodied **cobra** hanging over my club. With a big grin, he handed the club to me. I nearly passed out. What was I meant to do with it? I gave it straight back to him with instructions to throw it into the long rough, which he did, although it was the short rough so poor flight behind me.

After that, I hit a ten and my game disintegrated completely. Carlos tried his best to calm me down, without much luck, so we decided to abandon the round and retire to the clubhouse, where I had a very stiff brandy. But I did give my caddy a generous tip as he had undoubtedly saved my life, I'm sure. I doubt whether *cobras* are too keen at having metal spikes stuck in them! I rarely used my nine iron after that, preferring my pitching wedge instead. Shame, but I just couldn't get the vision of this dangling reptile out of my mind for ages.

During Peter and Andrée's mid-tour leave in 1978, I did manage a trip to Papua New Guinea (PNG) for five days with Carlos for the PNG Open Golf Tournament, PNG having just joined the Asia-Pacific Golf Confederation. He was playing, and I was entered as an ever-hopeful amateur. We flew to Port Moresby, then up country to Lae, where the tournament was being held. We stayed with some friends of his, but the stay was marred by their servant stealing a gold locket Mum and Dad had given me, which upset me greatly.

Once at the course, I was just about to tee off when a Lady Official came hurrying up to me saying I had to change my golf skirt because it was too short and would excite the Papuans! I'd had no problems with my attire in the Philippines, but obviously here things were different. I dashed into the Ladies Locker Room and put on the skirt I had come in, a mid-calf straight denim one, which was all I had and was completely unsuitable for golf as it restricted my swing and was incredibly hot in the humidity. I struggled round the course as best I could and, amazingly, came fifth – no thanks to the skirt.

On my way back to the UK at the end of my tour in Manila, I stayed for four days in the idyllic Seychelles, where I even managed to play a round of golf on my own on the nine-hole course at the hotel.

Here I encountered danger of a different sort – c*oconuts*! The fairly narrow fairways were lined with coconut palms, and dodging falling coconuts became something of an art and a necessity as they weigh a lot and will kill you if they land on your head! No deviation from the fairway here: straight down the middle, or nothing. I did manage to complete the round, but I can't say it was restful. However, a large glass of white wine relaxing on my patio gazing over a turquoise, shimmering India Ocean seemed to restore my peace and tranquility very nicely.

Not conducive to a relaxing round of golf!

I did join *La Planicie* Golf Club in **Lima** and enjoyed many a round there with my ex-pat friends. Fortunately, the only hazards here were lizards. I could cope with them, having survived scorpions and geckos in the Philippines.

There was no sport at all for me in **Guatemala**, sadly.

I wasn't grand enough to join the prestigious golf club in **Mexico City**: only the Ambassador could do so. He didn't play, but was not allowed to transfer his membership over, so I had to play where I could out of the DF. Our Security Officer, Syd Richardson, was the only other member of the Embassy who played golf, so he and his wife Jen and I used to take off at weekends into the mountains to play at a little hotel course at Ixtapan de la Sal. I loved these trips with them. It wasn't a very challenging course, but was pleasant, surrounded by mountains. If Syd were alive today he would smile if I mentioned 'my lazy eight'. He used to tease me about it as that was all I needed to reach the green on the par threes.

But do not be complacent, Gillian. When I drove down to Acapulco, a ten-hour obstacle course through the mountains, if I had time I went a bit further up the coast to Ixtapa, where there was another golf course. On my first visit, again I was playing on my own, and was enjoying the sultry breeze and the lakes on the course when I happened to spot a sign which did not fill me with glee.

Please do not disturb the crocodiles. No chance!

'*Favor de no molestar a los crocodrilos*'   (Please do not disturb the crocodiles)

Oh no. Surely not. Not content with being bitten by a **cobra**, I was now about to get eaten by a **crocodile.** I queried this with my caddy, who assured me that they had just eaten (who, I'm not quite sure) and would not be a problem. I wasn't convinced. Caddies have a knack of distorting the truth sometimes. But I was determined to press on, though I did have a scare when I was tee-ing off and stared straight into the steely eyes of a large crocodile basking in the sun on the edge of my tee. Needless to say, I shanked my tee shot straight into the lake. Well, I wasn't going to look for that ball. I had no wish to meet up with his relatives. Funny how many balls I lost on that round!

I loved my golf in **Hungary.**

The Budapest Golf Club, later renamed the Hungarian Golf Club, was founded in 1910, and Hungarian golf played a major role in European golf between 1926 and 1936. However, after the War it became the subject of political discrimination in the country and was considered an undesirable sport. Despite attempts to revive it, it wasn't until 1976 that Dr Ference Gáti, an agricultural engineer, started its rebirth by founding the *Kek Duna* (Blue Danube) Golf Club, situated on an island in the middle of the Danube, to which I belonged. It was a slow process, and the majority of players when I was there were ex-pats and diplomats. Between 1982 and 1989 golf was a section of the Field Hockey Association, and it was only in 1989, just before I arrived, that the Hungarian Golf Association was formed.

I played as often as I could, with some eminent opponents (cf Prince Andrew). My best friend was Lola Ryan, a member of the US Embassy, and we were out playing nearly every weekend in the summer, the course being closed from November to March because of the harsh winters.

My moment of glory came in 1991 when, after a fierce tussle with Lola, I became the Hungarian Ladies Open Champion and received a very handsome trophy. The standard was not that high, and my handicap was only eight, but at least I won!

Hockey

From the age of eleven, when I played on the wing in Dad's Mixed Hockey Team, to captaining my school hockey team, then playing for Leicestershire County and Midlands 'B', I have always loved hockey and, forgive the immodesty, have been fairly good at it. I did miss it so much for many years because of my sea-going career and the countries to which I was first posted, but I couldn't believe my luck when I arrived in Chile and found that hockey was a popular sport in that country, having arrived there in the middle of the twentieth century, mainly through the influence of ex-pats.

My first objective when I arrived in Chile, therefore, was to join the very exclusive Prince of Wales Country Club in Santiago. I had to have an interview to be accepted, but at least I had a diplomatic discount on the subscription, which helped, but not by much, as it was very expensive. But to me, it was worth every peso.

Craighouse Old Girls Hockey Team, Santiago,
with Rodrigo, our excellent coach.

The Club had the most amazing and successful Ladies hockey team, Craighouse Old Girls, and whilst I wasn't an Old Girl of that prestigious school, I quickly became a supernumerary aunt so I could join. We won the First League, and even went on tour, though I was mortified that I wasn't allowed by the Ambassador to go with them to Argentina just after the Falklands. Not a good idea, Gillian, he said. He did have a point!

Tennis

I also loved tennis, having played a lot too before I went to sea. At most of my Posts, there was no dedicated tennis club, so I ended up playing at friends' houses if they were lucky enough to have a court. In Mexico City , I managed to join a country club at *Satelite,* on the outskirts of the DF, and went there when I could if I wasn't playing golf. The members were mostly ex-pats, and I made some good friends through my tennis.

As I wrote to Mum and Dad (both keen tennis players too):

"Tennis going great guns here. My Pro is a bagful of energy, whilst I'm still trying to find my altitude legs and get used to the decompressed balls which fly through the air at something approaching Concorde speed. Consequently, most of mine go out of court! But we are winning slowly, and my acquired bad habits are starting to disappear.

"Maybe I'll make next year's Davis Cup Team! Next week it's the turn of the Aussies v Mexico. I'm desperately trying to charm my colleagues from Down Under to get me a ticket. Well, they did invite me to their National Day Reception, and I do send a regular supply of British sausages (made specially by a British lady living here) to the Aussie Ambassador each week as he's very partial to them.

"So, no ticket, no more sausages."

Needless to say, I did get a ticket, and the Aussie Ambassador continued to munch his way happily through many more packets of sausages. Oh, the feeling of power!

Swimming
Again, I love swimming, so I took the opportunity to do so at the Residences or friends' houses whenever I could.

Skiing
Having arrived back in the UK unexpectedly after Guatemala, on learning I was being posted to Chile, I wanted to find out as much as I could about living there, and so read extensively. One of the things I did discover was that there was excellent skiing at Portillo, in the heart of the Andes surrounded by high peaks. The season is from June to September. It's a bit of a trek to get there, being 141 kms by

road (84 kms direct), and we needed snow chains, but that wouldn't deter my colleagues or me.

The problem was: I didn't ski!

So, I decided to take myself off to the dry ski slope at Woolwich to learn. Easier said than done: it proved to be a rather painful experience! I was thirty-six at this stage, and afraid of falling, which didn't augur well for this sport, but I stuck at it and felt confident I could at least manage the baby slopes when I got to Chile. I bought all the gear and was much looking forward to this new challenge.

Skiing at Semmering, Austria (from Budapest)

But I wasn't very good, spending much of my time on my *derrière*. I kept going in Chile, and again when posted to Budapest. There were some good skiers in the Embassy and, ever hopeful, I would go with them to the slopes in Austria when I could. But I never did progress from the baby ones. I might look an expert but looks can be so deceptive! At least the gear looks professional, though!

Once back permanently in the UK after Hungary, I kept up my golf and tennis, though sadly I don't play all that much of either sport now. And with the advancing years, hockey is no longer a reality!

I loved every minute I spent on my sport whilst abroad. Wherever I was, it brought me many friendships and played an important part in my life. I have some truly great memories from it - and a few bruises! And, more to the point, I'm still in one piece, though I haven't lost my fear of snakes!

PART EIGHT
Around the World

Chapter Seventeen

A Snapshot of my Travels

I have been so lucky during my travelling career to have visited such a wealth of fascinating and spectacular locations, and my life has been all the richer for the mysteries and delights they have revealed, the friends I have made along the way, and the knowledge I have gained from my wanderings. My leave allowance wasn't all that generous, but I was determined to pack as much into my free time as I could. I never minded travelling on my own. There was always someone to talk to, and I could go where I liked, when I liked, which to me was, and still is, important.

To try to describe all my journeys would take forever, so I have selected just a few, which I hope will give you a flavour of where I have been and what I have done. As you can imagine, I have hundreds of photographs up in the loft to remind me of these adventures, but I only have room for a few here. I've divided my trips into regions, which I think will be easier to follow.

South-East Asia

Not only was the Philippines a wonderful country to be posted to, but it also gave me the chance to travel to other places in South-East Asia when I could. Golf gave me the excuse to visit PNG once again, but from my sea-going days **Hong Kong** had always been my favourite port and I couldn't wait to go there again.

I managed three short trips from Manila. The flight only took roughly two and a half hours, so it was do-able for a long weekend. I stayed on Kowloon-side in a hotel near the waterfront on Nathan Road, the oldest road in the Colony. The location was ideal. From there I used to hop on one of the many historic green and white Star Ferries at

Ocean Terminal, which I knew well, for the five-minute journey across Victoria Harbour to the Central District. Once there, I used to wander to my heart's content along West Connaught Road, through the Tiger Balm Gardens, or take the Tram up to The Peak. A bus trip round the island via Repulse Bay was also a must.

The bustling side streets of Kowloon were always a magnet too, and I managed to locate my old tailor from my P&O days who had made me two fabulous silk outfits (complete with boots) which I had worn at our fashion parades on board. I'm not sure he remembered me, but we chatted away like old friends. I didn't need anything making now, but it was good to see him again. It was very rare for me to come away with nothing, though. Just as well I was limited on baggage size and weight!

The iconic sampan

Would I visit Hong Kong today? No. It bears little resemblance to the destination I loved so much, and I can well empathize with Sir Chris Patten as he wept when he sailed away at the end of his Governorship. I do so fear for the **HKSAR** (Hong Kong Special Administrative Region of the People's Republic of China). All I can do is wish the inhabitants well.

As I've already described, travelling to and from Manila also gave me the opportunity to stop off in New Delhi, Sri Lanka, Singapore, the Seychelles, and Hawaii. There were, of course, my many trips within the Philippines too, so I feel I benefitted well from my time there.

Central and South America

Yet again, I was fortunate in my postings to South America as it gave me the chance to explore that wonderful Continent further.

Starting in **Peru**, how could I not go to *Machu Picchu*? I had the opportunity to spend five days in that region when the Ambassador was himself away travelling. I flew up to Cusco, once the homeland of the Incas, and made that my base from where to explore the surrounding area. It was truly memorable: the Inca ruins at *Sacsayhuamán*, the *Moray* stone circles, and the living Inca town of *Ollantytambo*.

An Inca family at Ollantaytambo

When it was time to go up to *Machu Picchu*, I caught the little train that huffed and puffed as it wound its way round the mountainside and got off at the tiny station halfway up. From there, with a rucksack on my back, I hiked the rest of the way to the

Sanctuary Lodge, where I was staying. Getting a room here was like gold dust. It was the only place to stay at the site, and I had had to book well in advance: it certainly wasn't cheap either. It used to be a scientists' hut, but I couldn't have asked for a more magical location.

The Lodge only took six guests. We all left together at four am with our guide, torches in hand, to see the sunrise over the Andes, striking *Intihuatana* (the Hitching Post of the Sun). The route was slightly treacherous, negotiating sleeping llamas on the way, but the experience was beyond words. The stillness, the sound of the Urubamba River, source of the Amazon River, roaring through the gorge below. It was so, so beautiful. Because of the difficult time I was having in Lima, I just sat there and cried.

Machu Picchu

Though my stay in Peru was much shorter than I wanted, I did manage to visit *Arequipa,* with its historic Santa Catalina Convent, and the *Reserva Nacional de Paracas* (the largest area of protected coastline in Peru).

My three-day excursion to the **Amazon Basin** was so very different from anything I had experienced before. I had to fly to **Iquitos**, the largest city in the Basin, as there was no road access, only river and air, and the heat and humidity hit me as soon as I stepped off the plane.

In 1980 tourism hadn't yet taken much of a hold in this region, so the best thing to do was to take tours, the most memorable of which were a trip down the Amazon River, and into the rain forest.

On the river, I was rather apprehensive to say the least in case I met one of ***Albert's*** relatives. I doubt they wouldn't take too kindly if they knew that a distant cousin was now stuffed and hanging on a wall. Piranhas I could cope with: anacondas, definitely not. Fortunately, these enormous reptiles stayed well clear, obviously not wanting to be a wall decoration themselves!

We didn't venture too far into the forest, but I did manage to catch a glimpse of flamboyant macaws and parrots (no swearing here), and a few spider monkeys. And I do remember being frightened out of my wits when, looking into a raised tank, up surfaced a friendly *paice* (pronounced pie-chay), the world's largest freshwater fish which can grow to more than ten feet long and weight over four hundred and forty pounds. We rubbed 'snouts', he puffed in my face, and was gone. He might not have been dangerous, but he certainly was **BIG**.

In **Guatemala** it wasn't possible to venture far, of course, but **Chile** proved to be an excellent 'base' for some fascinating trips. Within the country, one way or another I travelled the whole length of it, all four thousand or so miles, either flying, by train or driving. The Pan-

American Highway covered much of the length, but I had to fly from Puerto Montt if I wanted to reach Punta Arenas, which I did with Pam.

I flew up to Arica, in the far north of Chile, where I hired a taxi with three Americans and visited *Lago Chungará*, close to the Bolivian border in the *Lauca* National Park. At fourteen thousand, eight hundred and forty feet, it is one of the highest lakes in the world, formed when the *Volcán Parinacota* collapsed and the debris from the collapse dammed the *Lauca* River. I certainly did suffer from *soroche* at this altitude, so much so that I had difficulty breathing and the taxi driver, who had no oxygen cylinders with him, had to drive fairly rapidly to a lower altitude. The Americans didn't fare much better either.

The *Volcán Parinacota*, and *Lago Chungará*

Next was a journey into the Atacama Desert, staying at Calama. Whilst there, I was keen to see the geysers at *El Tatio*, one hundred and eighty-six kms away. The only way to do this was to hire a taxi, whose driver would act as my guide, which I did. Sr Ugalde was wonderful, and so was his wife, whom he had thoughtfully brought along for company as I was a female on her own.

The three of us set off around 2 am, across punishing desert terrain, there being no roads, only tracks, to the interior to see this thermal; phenomenon which only happened around dawn. The Ugalde's had brought with them two flasks of coffee, bottles of water, some *marraquetas* (also known as *pan francés*) filled with jam, and oranges, so we had breakfast in the eerily quiet pitch black desert and waited for the sun to rise. The geysers were dramatic, steam soaring high into the sky, and although they only lasted for about half an hour, the spectacle was well worth seeing. Apart from a mild attack of *soroche* again, I really enjoyed the trip, as well as Sr and Sra Ugalde's company and kindness.

El Tatio (difficult to photo, though, because of the steam)

The next day I caught the bus to travel the one hundred kms to the arid town of San Pedro de Atacama to see the 'Copper Man' mummy dating from c. 550 AD, and other artifacts. Then back to Calama, stopping off at the salt flats on the way. Interesting.

I had been looking forward so much to the next day. The Ambassador had arranged for me to pay a visit to the **Chuquicamata**

(*Chuqui* for short) **Copper Mine**, only seventeen kms away from Calama.

Its history is fascinating. Mining in this area dates back to the pre-colonial Incas (this is where the 'Copper Man' mummy was found) and the Spanish *Conquistadores*. After that, the site was mined by both Chilean and English companies from 1879-1912, and was then owned by Anaconda Copper (that name again!). It is now run by Codelco, a Chilean state enterprise.

I was staggered by its size. At nine thousand three hundred feet, it's the largest open-pit **excavated** copper mine in the world (Bingham Canyon Mine in Utah being the largest and deepest open-pit mine). I took a taxi from Calama to the site, and was warmly welcomed by the Manager, who had organized one of his staff to take me on a guided tour after a short film explaining their operation. I was fascinated and was thrilled to bits when they started dynamiting. I love dynamiting! And I couldn't believe the size of the ore-carrying trucks. The Manager kindly invited me to stay for lunch, which I accepted, and arranged for a taxi to take me back to Calama.

At the Chuquicamata Copper Mine

The Ambassador and our First Secretary Commercial were most interested to hear how I had got on at *Chuqui*. They were delighted that I had been interested enough to want to pay a visit to the mine, and that I had been looked after so well. All part of furthering Anglo-Chilean relations, they said. In my own small way, I was pleased to help.

I was sad to leave Calama the next day, but I had to get back, so I took another bus to Iquique and caught a flight back to Santiago. It had been a long and tiring trip, but I loved every minute of it, and had learned so much along the way.

Still in Chile, the Ambassador was taking some leave one Christmas, and so said I could do so too. I had heard about a wonderful little ship, **SKORPIOS 1**, which used to sail from Puerto Montt through the Chilean fjords and down to the glacier *San Rafael*. She was only one hundred and sixty-four feet one inch long (don't know how they measured the one inch), had four decks, took sixty-eight passengers, and had an average speed of ten knots, not quite CANBERRA but that mattered not one bit. I really wanted to sail in her. Trying to get a cabin, especially at Christmas, was very difficult, but I rang up on the off-chance and was overjoyed to find there had just been a cancellation and so I could take that cabin. I flew down to Puerto Montt and couldn't contain my excitement as I stepped aboard.

Mv *SKORPIOS*

She was lovely. She had a simple wooden interior, and the cabins were very basic, but I didn't mind at all. Captain Kochifas was quite a character: a mine of information, and great fun. He was so impressed that I had a Steering Certificate from my P&O days that he let me steer in the wider channels. Brave man! I was in my element. My fellow passengers were very congenial too, and we had a riotous Christmas. I made friends with the other two solo travellers on board: Richard, an elderly American, and Jean-Paul, a Frenchman a bit younger than me. We got on really well together, which made the voyage even more enjoyable.

The Chilean Lake District is so beautiful, and for one week we sailed in and out of tiny coves between the **Isla Grande de Chiloé** and the mighty Pacific Ocean. The weather was excellent, and we moored at the small towns of Chiloé and Castro, taking a dip in the thermal baths there. Eventually we reached the *Laguna San Rafael* and anchored near the foot of the enormous glacier. From there we went out in the ship's two lifeboats, navigating between ice bergs, making sure we didn't go too close inshore to avoid the large waves caused by parts of the glacier breaking off. It was thrilling. We even had a small glass of whisky on two-thousand-year-old 'rocks' to celebrate. But a mist came down suddenly, so we had to return to the ship quickly in case we got trapped amongst the ice. Again, this was such a special adventure, and the memories of that week will stay with me forever too.

At the Ventisquero (glacier) San Rafael

Continuing with a water theme, but travelling further afield this time, I was also able to pay a four-day visit to Paraguay, ostensibly to visit the *Iguazu Falls* . I loved Asunción, but the *Falls* are something else.

First of all, the noise. It's absolutely deafening. And then the image of that immense weight of water pouring over the cliffs. I kept thinking of the opening scene of *'The Mission'*, filmed here. How must those Jesuit priests have felt during the Guaraní War when, as a punishment, they were thrown into the raging river, only to plummet to their death over the cliff edge into the boiling cauldron below. I truly hope their Faith sustained them.

I stayed on the Paraguayan side which gives the best view, so they say. I got soaked from the clouds of spray, of course, but that didn't matter. In the end, I took my life into my own hands and walked with a tightly controlled group to the end of the walkway looking down into the *Garganta del Diablo.* I must be a glutton for punishment. I can't tell you how frightening that was.

I spent the night at the Das Cataratas Hotel at Iguazu. It was difficult to sleep for the noise, but I will never, ever, forget *Iguazu Falls* .

Iguazu Falls, from the Paraguayan Side
I stood on the end of that walkway. Absolutely petrifying. And wet!

There were also other trips from Chile - to Costa Rica, and back to Lima for a quick visit. Each very enjoyable

I didn't venture out of **Mexico**. There was so much to see and do in that captivating country that there was no need. Acapulco beckoned (often), and I managed visits to Vera Cruz and Oaxaca, as well as out and about around the DF. Life couldn't have been better.

My years in South America with The Office afforded me some wonderful opportunities to travel, for which I have been extremely grateful.

Europe

From a travelling point of view, the timing of my posting to **Hungary** couldn't have been more opportune. The fall of Communism gave me access to countries I would otherwise have been denied as I was not allowed to visit a Communist country unless I was posted there. This was particularly galling in Mexico, where I was desperate to visit Cuba, but was forbidden to do so (I have been there twice since I retired and loved it). I was determined, therefore, to make the most of my time in Budapest, and with the judicious use of my leave allowance, plus the Ambassador's penchant for travelling, I was able to accomplish a lot.

Nothing brought home to me the stark reality of living under an unforgiving, repressive Communist regime more than my four-day visit to **Romania** from 8-11 October 1992. Although this was still Eastern Europe, the contrast with Hungary was striking, and alarming.

As our leave coincided, our Admin Officer (Sheila), Liz (DA's wife), Debbie (Second Sec Commercial), and I decided to visit the Painted Monasteries of Bukovina, part of Moldavia, a region in north-east Romania. Clustered around the city of Suceava, the *'Holy Eight'*, as they are known, are Romanian Orthodox Churches whose exterior walls are decorated with stunning fifteenth and sixteenth century frescoes depicting portraits of prophets and saints, scenes from the

214

life of Jesus, and images of angels and demons, heaven and hell. To me, they remind me of my time in Venice and Dante's *'Infierno'*. Considered masterpieces of Byzantine art, they are one of the most unique architectural sites of Europe. As with our own churches, the purpose of these scenes was to make the stories of the Bible known to villagers, who could neither read nor write (you can still see the remains of such murals in my own church of St Mary's). Seven of the churches were placed on the UNESCO's World Heritage list in 1993. The eighth, *Sucevita,* is awaiting agreement to be added to the list. Considering they are external walls in a harsh climate, the colours are truly remarkable.

The Painted Monasteries of Bukovina

The Monastery of SUCEVITA

Because of the lack of unleaded petrol in Romania, we all had to squash somehow into Debbie's slightly aging right-hand drive Vauxhall Cavalier. Easier said than done, as we were taking with us not only our big bags, but also a few emergency rations and a spare can of petrol – just in case. But as Debbie's car ran on leaded petrol, we felt this wouldn't be a problem. Really? We were in for a big shock.

We had booked two rooms at the rather foreboding Hotel *Castel Dracula* at Bistrita, up in the mountains near the ski centre. It was going to be a good ten-hour drive to get there, so we set off very early, crossing the Romanian border at Nădlac-Nagylak. We encountered a fair amount of hassle by the Romanian officials, who scrutinized our documents with a fine-tooth comb, but we were allowed to proceed on our way, though it was clear that our journey was going to be 'monitored' closely. We headed for Cluj Napoca, four hundred and sixty-seven kms away, taking it in turns to do the driving. However, on the way we needed to stop for petrol. We came to the only petrol station we had seen in miles, to be welcomed by a queue of at least two miles. Now what? If we joined the end of the queue, it would take us hours to get through so, having diplomatic number plates, we plucked up courage and went straight to the front.

Understandably, there was nearly a riot, and it was only the begrudging intervention of the police that saved us from serious physical harm. It was very frightening and brought back to me the nightmare of Guatemala. We genuinely felt guilty at queue-jumping, but terribly sad also. If this is what it had been like under Communism and Ceausescu in particular, heaven help the Romanians.

We filled the car and the spare can, and got out of there as quickly as possible, insults being hurled at us from every quarter. From that moment on, we were in a marked car. Our notoriety had obviously preceded us! Every few miles on the way to Cluj we were pulled over, asked for our documents again, and the car was searched. This was taking ages, and by now we were tired, hungry, and still had another two hours to go to Bistrita from Cluj.

Eventually we arrived in the dark at the weirdest hotel I've ever stayed at. The Trip Advisor reviews bore no resemblance to what we

The hotel *Castel Dracula*

encountered in 1993. We had taken our own washbasin plugs, as one had to do in most former Communist countries, but that wouldn't have made any difference because there was no pipe from the basin, so the water went all over the floor. The sheets were damask tablecloths; there were vampire logos all over the walls and doors; the wardrobe door dropped off; and to our horror we discovered there was virtually no food at all. We, and the few other guests, had to dine on dry bread, a boiled egg, greasy soup with bits floating in it, a biscuit, and a glass of water. Fortunately, we had brought a jar of coffee with us, but there was no milk, and when we asked for boiling water, this was frowned on.

Getting food and petrol during our visit was to prove a major problem. There were long queues at all the petrol stations we passed. We daren't risk another confrontation, and so had to rely on the goodwill of villagers who supplied us with black market petrol of dubious quality out of buckets at exorbitant prices. There were no supermarkets: only the Romanian equivalent of the *czem,* but there was little in them anyway. We just had to improvise and take what kind people gave us out of pity. Some nuns were very generous and shared some fruit and a piece of cake with us. But we were starved!

We had planned to make the *Castel Dracula* our base, but one night there was enough. We couldn't get away quick enough and decided to try our luck with a hotel in Suceava. We found one - basic, but a vast improvement, thankfully, though that wasn't too difficult.

On the way to Suceava, we met the amazing Grant Family. We came across this gypsy caravan with a WWF Panda placard on the back. We overtook it slowly, but when the occupants saw our diplomatic plates, they waved and shouted for us to stop. We did, and they caught up. It turned out this was Dad David, Mum Kate, and their three children: Torcuil, 17, Eilidh 16, and Fiona 13. They were from the Orkneys, and in 1990 had decided to sell up and circumnavigate the world in a horse-drawn caravan. They were so thrilled to see us and we spent about half an hour chatting away. But we had to get on, and sadly left them to continue on their way.

The Grant family horse-drawn caravan

Having spent a slightly more comfortable night at our new hotel in Suceava, the next morning we set off to visit the Monasteries some twenty miles or so away. It was a beautiful day, and the sun glinted off the walls, illuminating the vibrant colours of the frescoes that adorned them. They were magnificent.

We only managed to visit three in the time we had left - *Moldovita*, *Sucevita* and *Voronet* - but each one was breathtaking in its beauty, and more than compensated for the hassle and aggravation we were encountering on our journeys.

After two days it was time to return home. A change of plan meant that we now headed for Timisoara instead of back to Bistrita. We found a small, reasonably comfortable hotel in the centre of the city, and had a meal of sorts at last: bread and scrambled eggs. Never have eggs tasted so good! Again, though, there was nothing in the shops apart from yet more bread and the odd tin of meat. We bought what we could to last us on our way back, which fortunately was not too long as we were near to the Hungarian border. Miraculously, this part of our journey was uneventful: the officials had obviously found someone else to hassle.

Once back at the Embassy, everyone was clamouring to hear how we had got on, but details of our adventure could wait. First, we had to **EAT**!

Apart from the Monasteries, I was distressed by what I had seen and experienced in Romania. So backward a country, so downtrodden its people. I could only be thankful that the era of Communism was at an end and pray for a much brighter and happier future for them.

The legacy of Communism

Moving on, I remained undaunted by my experience in Romania. It takes a lot to daunt **me**!

Again, I used some of my leave to drive down through **Croatia**,*en route* to **Slovenia**, stopping off at **Zagreb** for a night. I was pleasantly surprised by this city, with its eighteenth and nineteenth century Austro-Hungarian architecture. Upper Town is the site of the Cathedral and St Marks Church, both of which I really liked. The country was also just beginning to open up after Communism, but I found it much more advanced and friendly than Romania.

From Zagreb I drove on to Ljubljana to see my great friend Erwan, from my Mexico days. He had been EU Ambassador there and was now EU Ambassador to Slovenia and much enjoying his new posting. It was so good to see him again (he later came to stay with me in Budapest). We spent time catching up, but he was frantically busy, so I travelled on to **Bled** where I stayed two nights, then back to Hungary.

I was very impressed with Slovenia, and its people. The countryside is very picturesque, and the people kind and courteous, which made quite a change. And Bled and its Lake are really quite special. Encircled by high mountains, the views all around are stunning, and I so enjoyed my walk along the shores the lake, although it was quite a way. I climbed up to the castle, and took a boat trip out to *Blejski Otok* Island to the Pilgrimage Church of the Assumption of Maria, where I rang the bell for good luck. It was a very enjoyable trip altogether and I was so glad I had been.

Then the same intrepid four of us crammed into Debbie's Cavalier once again to drive through the newly renamed **Czech Republic** to **Warsaw**, where we were staying with a friend of Debbie's in the Embassy. I loved the **Tatra Mountains,** and our stay for two nights in **Krakow**. Such a beautiful town. But I was much affected by my visit to Auschwitz and had nightmares about it for months afterward.

However, I do think people should go there: just to appreciate how cruel people can be to each other.

Seeing the horrors of that camp reminded me of Walter Rauff, inventor of the portable gas oven, who had been given sanctuary in Chile after the War. He lived, I believe, at secretive *Colonia Dignidad* near Valdivia, and died on 14 May 1984 of lung cancer and a heart attack during my posting there. It is thought that, under Pinochet, he may have been an adviser to the Chilean Secret Police, the DNA. I can well imagine that to be true. He must have been in his element.

The journey through Katowice to **Warsaw** was difficult with so many dilapidated commercial vehicles clogging up the road, but I liked the old part of the city once we arrived. Our time was limited, though, and we had to do the homeward journey in one go. I drew the short straw and had to drive through the Mountains during the night, which was really tiring and not a little fraught. But we made it. And we hadn't starved this time!

Wanting to broaden my knowledge of the region still further, I plucked up courage and made another sortie east – this time to **Serbia** via Szeged. Our First Sec Commercial in Budapest had been posted there midway through my own tour, and, once settled, he and his wife had invited Sheila and I to spend a weekend with them, which we were delighted to do. We went in Sheila's car this time, the unleaded petrol situation not being quite so dire as in Romania. It was great to see them again and it was a fascinating trip, though I still found the atmosphere rather hostile and the inhabitants aggressive towards foreigners. The one thing I remember most of all, though, was going to an Orthodox Church and listening to the monks chanting. It was so beautiful, and powerful.

I flew on my own up to **Prague** to spend three days there. Again, a beautiful city. And over a period of a few months, I made the short journey of about an hour and a half to a famous crystal factory just over the border with **Slovakia** as I was buying, in stages, a beautiful set of Bohemian cut glass wine, spirits and liqueur glasses at a very reasonable price. As soon as I had saved up enough for the next set, off I went. I still have some of it. I didn't get a chance to see much of the country on these trips, though I did drive twice from Vienna to Bratislava, which seemed very pleasant in places, with a few attractive buildings, but a bit uninspiring generally.

Apart from these longer excursions, when I could, I went out and about around Hungary. *Lake Balaton* was a popular destination, as was *Visegrad* and the *Danube Bend,* where I took Mum and Dad. It was interesting to visit the wine growing region of *Tokay* too - even better to sample the excellent wine produced there!

The End of My Diplomatic Travels

I was sad to leave Hungary. I hadn't looked forward to my posting there but had been surprised at how much I had come to enjoy and appreciate that country: perhaps some of the people in the region a little less so. I had worked so hard, but had also made the most of the time and the opportunities for travel that my stay had afforded me, and I felt satisfied that I had 'given it my best shot'.

Eventually my tour came to an end, and I returned to the UK for another home posting, certain in the knowledge that I would have at least one (hopefully Madrid), if not two, more postings before I retired.

But few things in this life are ever certain. Dear Dad's death meant I needed to stay at home with Mum, which I was more than happy to do, so I reluctantly accepted that I'd go travelling with The Office no more. It was the end of an era for me. Tough to come to terms with, but I was (and am) so grateful for all that I had/have been privileged enough to see and do over the last thirty years as a member of the Diplomatic Service.

Thank you so much, FCO. One thing **is** certain, though. I wouldn't have changed the life you gave me for the world.

PART NINE

New Horizons

Chapter Eighteen

New Horizons

Farewell FCO

On 5 July 2001, I completed twenty-five years of loyal service with The Office, and to mark the occasion a small reception was held for me to celebrate this achievement. My boss, John Macgregor, presented me with a beautiful, framed certificate in recognition of my years of dedication, which I still prize highly: it was a proud moment.

However, as time progressed, the day I had been dreading for so long fast approached, until at last it arrived. I remember it so clearly. It was a Wednesday. 16 April 2005. My sixtieth birthday. The day I legally had to retire from the Diplomatic Service. I wasn't even allowed to see the week out.

As I walked under the arch into the Quadrangle and climbed the steps of the Main Entrance for the last time that morning, so many thoughts, images, memories came flooding back to me: meeting Ambassador Karasin, and so many other visitors on these same steps; my postings; the hazardous and difficult times I had experienced; the camaraderie of my colleagues. Now all that would be gone.

It was such a difficult day. I didn't do much work, I have to admit, but my boss, Clare Smith, knew how emotional I was and asked someone else to take over my job. This gave me time to go around The Office saying goodbye to those whom I knew who were on leave or on a home posting. We reminisced. They were very sad to see me go, they all said, and wished me well. I cleared my office, put all my things in a plastic bag, said goodbye to Clare, and closed my door.

At 8.50 am I had arrived at my place of work as a proud member of Her Majesty's Diplomatic Service. At 5 pm I walked through the arch again, a proud member of – nothing. A nobody. Like a mariner destined to be marooned forever on a ship without a rudder, staring across a vast expanse of ocean with no land in sight. I was ready for the breaker's yard, just like my beloved CANBERRA and ORIANA.

In a daze I made my way down Victoria Street to the station, and sat alone on the train home to Wallington, where I now lived.

When I arrived at my empty flat, I just closed the door – and wept.

New Horizons

My next few weeks as a retired person were tough. Mum and Dad were no longer alive; Sheila had her family up north in Wigan. How was I going to fill my lonely, meaningless days? I just knew I had to get out of this self-pitying mindset quickly and move on.

And I did. My salvation came in July in the form of an advert in the Chichester Observer looking for a Registration Service Usher. Just up my street I thought. I would belong to another prestigious organization, be able to meet people and have a role to play in their lives. I applied, was immediately accepted, and after two years I was asked if I would become a Registrar, which I did.

And this is where I am today. Still working hard aged seventy-seven, and absolutely loving my job once again. When conducting Citizenship Ceremonies, I have even found my time with The Office invaluable as I have been able to empathize, and communicate well with our new Citizens. As an added bonus, I work with the most amazing colleagues yet again. So, I'm as happy as a sand boy!

And what of the future?

Well, this little butterfly's wings are still fluttering. Not quite as fast as they once did, perhaps, but they are still propelling her forward, nonetheless. I'm off to Antigua in December. I wonder what Miss Lofting would have made of that?

"You're rather old to be going there now, Gillian", I can hear her say.

"Not at all, Miss Lofting. As you know, we FCO PAs are an intrepid bunch. Remember, resilience and flexibility are the name of the game. I'm afraid I'm rather too old to change now."

I think the Monarch butterflies would have understood, don't you.

New Horizons
My new life as a Registrar

Acknowledgements

After the success of my memoir *'From Oceans to Embassies'*, which brought back so many happy memories for me, and readers seemed to enjoy, I was then asked if I could go into more detail about my career in the Diplomatic Service in particular. I've been more than happy to do so, and the result is this, my new book, *'Skirting the World'*.

There are certain people whose help and advice have been invaluable to me whilst pounding away at the keyboard. I would like to thank my former colleagues who dug deep into their memories to clarify certain points; and looked over relevant chapters for me to make sure I didn't reveal things I shouldn't have revealed! You know who you are, and I'm most grateful.

My thanks in particular go to Mark Bertram for all his help; to the Curator of the GCHQ Museum; and to Beth Ellis and Susie Cox at P&O Heritage, for allowing me to use certain photographs, which add to my story. Also, to my New Zealand friend, Colin Wilson, for his constant support; to David Parsons at my excellent printers, Imprint Digital, whom I know I can always rely on for his technical help; and to Helen Christmas at Cottagewebs for designing my book cover, which I think looks extremely good.

It can be a bit lonely sometimes being an author, but the encouragement I've received whilst writing this book is much appreciated, particularly from my lifelong friends Marie, Sue and Pam, and my family. I've worked almost as hard as I did for the FCO, often through the night, to put down on paper my thoughts, experiences, recollections, and reflections from my time in the Diplomatic Service. I've so enjoyed re-living my life and hope my readers will find it interesting. However, I can't help heaving a sigh of relief that I've finished it. Perhaps now I can get a decent night's sleep at last!